Japan

Japan

MARTIN HÜRLIMANN
FRANCIS KING

A STUDIO BOOK
THE VIKING PRESS · NEW YORK

THE TEXTS BY MARTIN HÜRLIMANN
TRANSLATED FROM THE GERMAN
BY D. J. S. THOMSON

© Copyright 1970 by Thames and Hudson Ltd and Martin Hürlimann
All rights reserved

Published in 1970 by The Viking Press, Inc.
625 Madison Avenue, New York, N. Y. 10022

SBN 670-40572-8

Library of Congress catalog card number: 73-100603

Gravure illustrations printed in Switzerland by Imago, Zurich
Text printed in Germany by Boss-Druck, Kleve
Bound in Holland by Van Rijmenam N.V., The Hague

CONTENTS

JAPAN AND ITS PEOPLE

Many Japanese tourists have been heard to remark on the lack of trees to be found in Western countries. This may at first sight seem surprising, yet a visit to Japan soon serves to explain this apparent anomaly; for, apart from Hokkaido, the northern island, the three other main islands consist of tightly wooded hills and narrow valleys, of which the predominating colour is invariably green: the dark green of the firs, the grass-green of the rice, the light and dark green of the pines that are often silhouetted against a bottle-green sea. Travelling through Japan, one has the sensation of being an earwig crawling over one fold after another of a vast lettuce.

The actual area of Japan, though less than that of California, is almost twice that of Great Britain; but because of the steep, arboreous hills, only 16 per cent of the land is cultivable. In spite of this, today's population is 102 million, more than half that of the United States. The American Japanologist, Edward Seidensticker, once referred to Japan as 'this lonely, crowded country': a felicitous phrase not merely because the people are not spread over the land equally like butter on toast but are crushed into the valleys and along the coasts to leave the mountains free of habitation, but also because in no other country of the world can human beings live in such physical proximity to each other and yet remain so self-contained.

In the old days the Japanese never thought of putting anything on the crests of their forested hills other than a Buddhist temple or a Shinto shrine. It did not occur to them to crown the crests with villages or fortifications as in Greece or Italy or Spain; Nagasaki is one of the few ancient cities in Japan built over hills. But in recent years, as the population has swelled and swelled and the housing-shortage has become graver and graver, around every major city the bull-dozers have begun to sweep away the thick vegetation that clothes the surrounding slopes, in order that modern apartment blocks, often of an unparalleled ugliness and squalor, should supplant the bamboos, firs and pines.

The first view that the traveller has of Japan is usually of Tokyo; and a dispiriting one it is, as he drives from Haneda Airport through what appears to be a shanty-town afflicted with elephantiasis. Tokyo suffers from the same ills as every Western city of any size, but in an even more acute form: crowded public transport (student toughs who, in the West, might be earning money as chuckers-out are employed by the National Railways as pushers-in); traffic-jams; parking-problems; accidents; crimes of violence; garish advertisements; buildings like up-ended chests of drawers. Arriving in Tokyo for the first time, I might have been arriving in any huge industrial nexus in any part of the globe. True, there were ideograms everywhere; but apart from them, there was nothing particularly oriental about the main thoroughfares, the shopping centres, or the business quarters. The cinemas were showing the same films as in London or Paris or New York, the automobiles looked the same as anywhere (only at the bottom of the Ginza, near the Kabuki-za, did I see a *jinriksha*, pulled by an elderly man in traditional costume and containing a white-faced geisha), and in the shops the same sort of household items, cosmetics and clothes were on sale—even the models had Caucasian features and hair.

Yet when one leaves the principal streets of Tokyo, and wanders into the narrow lanes of the residential quarters, the pressure of life miraculously slackens, the pace slows, the all-pervasive ugliness vanishes. These districts, though they are in the heart of the city, have an oddly rural atmosphere. This is because Tokyo is really not a single city but a collection of towns and villages that have spread, melted into each other and so formed a complex maze. In these country towns and villages, each encapsulated within an intricate membrane of railway lines and roads and telephone wires and electricity cables, one at last feels that one is touching Japan. The noodle-seller trundles his cart down an ill-lit alley, halts and plays a few notes on his flute; shopkeepers in cotton kimono *(yukata)* stand outside their shops, gossiping to each other; people in clogs click-clack to and from the public-bath, clutching towel and soap.

Tokyo, literally 'The Eastern Capital', has only been the capital of Japan since 1868, when the Emperor Meiji moved from Kyoto, where his predecessors had lived for generations in splendid impotence, to take up residence in the palace of the overthrown shogun. In 1877 its population was only just half a million. Named after Shogun Yoritomo's political agent for the area, and founded towards the end of the twelfth century, it was known as Edo before the Meiji Restoration. People who were born in Tokyo and whose families have lived there for at least three generations qualify for the proud designation of Edoko (an Edo person). Of the old Edo, which forms the background to so many Kabuki plays, more than a trace, though rapidly disappearing, can still be found near the Shimbashi Embijo theatre and the great Fish Market, by the Sumida River, around Ueno Station and in the region of the Asakusa Kannon (Goddess of Mercy) Temple. To this last temple, famous in legend and literature, visitors from all over the country make their way to light joss-sticks, clap their hands and utter a prayer. Around it one finds a number of *sushi* shops, each with its sign in Chinese characters, its piece of split curtain over its sliding door and its unpolished but scrupulously scrubbed wood counter, behind which stand men with cloths wrapped round their heads, their hands deftly preparing wads of rice stuffed with raw fish and wrapped in seaweed. Around it too one may see—as I saw on my first visit—suddenly intermingling with the traffic of the city a *mikoshi* or gold and lacquered shrine palanquin, carried shoulder-high by a gang of yelling, grimacing youths, naked but for their exiguous loin-cloths. It is the festival of the local Shinto shrine and the youths of the district have been recruited to give the holy *mikoshi* an airing. Stimulated by draughts of *saké* provided for them en route, they carry out this task with fervid abandon, jogging the palanquin up and down with such vigour that one wonders that it does not disintegrate.

The entranced expressions on the faces of these *mikoshi* bearers suggest a religious fanaticism; but the majority of Japanese might be described as fanatics without a faith. They are a superstitious people but not a religious one. Every Japanese has been influenced by Buddhist culture, just as every Westerner has, willy-nilly, been influenced by Christianity, and many a Japanese home has a little Buddhist shrine in the corner of one of its rooms. In the same home there may also be a Shinto shrine, and the juxtaposition will seem odd to no one but a foreigner. One of my students would often proclaim to me, with an aggressiveness that was no doubt due to his mistaken belief that I was a missionary: 'I am atheist! Religion is opium of

I This type of monastery garden, devoid of vegetation, where the motif of the island surrounded by the ocean is created in sand and rock, the Japanese find particularly conducive to contemplation. Sangen-in, Kyoto.

people!' But when he eventually got married, I was invited to a ceremony performed by a Shinto priest; and when, tragically, his wife died in childbirth, her funeral, which I also attended, was according to the Buddhist rites.

Shinto—the Way of the Gods—was the native, animistic cult of Japan. Its chief deity is Amaterasu (the Sun Goddess), from whom the Emperor was supposed to descend, with innumerable attendant deities in a pantheon not merely of gods and goddesses of the sea, the rivers, winds, fire and mountains but also of deified persons. For Shinto to have survived the introduction of Buddhism and to continue, even today, to coexist with a system of beliefs so much more sophisticated and intellectual, is indeed remarkable. When Buddhism and the Confucian ethical code began to permeate Japan in the middle of the sixth century AD, Shinto gradually got mixed up with the new beliefs; but it never became completely absorbed, so that in the nineteenth century it could without difficulty be extricated from its entanglement with Buddhism (at one time Buddhist and Shinto priests officiated indifferently in both temples and shrines) and then, because of its assertions of the mythical birth of Japan and the divinity of the Emperor, be elevated into a nationalistic cult.

Although not a religious country—coming to it, St Francis Xavier is reported to have said that it is always easier to convert people who have had some prior religious belief rather than those who have none at all—Japan abounds in almost as many religious sects as universities. There are eleven main Buddhist ones and numerous offshoots, some of which—like the new religions of California—wither away on the death of their cranky founders. In recent years, however, a new Buddhist sect has appeared which looks like becoming influential and even dangerous. It is called Soka-gakkai (Value Creating Society). Founded before the war, with a membership of thousands, it can now claim millions of adherents, of whom the number increases vastly each year. Its principal saint is Nichiren, a thirteenth-century Buddhist evangelist, even though the members of the original Nichiren sect denounce Soka-gakkai for appropriating their founder. The ardour of the Soka-gakkai members was evidenced when an appeal for was made for money to finance the building of a temple near Mount Fuji, nearly four times the Sum asked being subscribed in four days. I myself had proof of this ardour on a train-journey between Kyoto and Matsue when, for the space of more than four hours, a schoolboy of thirteen or fourteen, incapable of speaking English, urged on me the merits of the new religion in a Japanese almost totally incomprehensible to me. I eventually left the train with a sheaf of pamphlets under my arm. Another friend of mine had the misfortune to fall into the hands of a Soka-gakkai taxi-driver who, during the murderous rush-hour in Tokyo, seemed more concerned over my friend's spiritual welfare than the protection of his person. Soka-gakkai has now entered politics, with members in both the Senate and the Lower House, and in the future its political influence seems certain to grow. The Japanese often feel lonely and fear loneliness and there are many lonely people in the cities (sabichi, meaning sad because one is lonely, is a word that crops up in almost every popular song). The chief cause of loneliness for a Japanese is to feel that he is a member of no gang, group or circle; so the attraction of a new, thriving and close-knit sect is precisely that it gives its adherents an assurance of belonging.

This desire to belong, which has as its natural complement a terror of being, whether physically or intellectually, left out in isolation, immediately strikes any visitor to Japan. In every Japanese railway station, as Arthur Koestler noted, you will see ant-like trails of people, each carrying a small banner in

II *Among Japan's still active volcanoes is the 4,900 foot-high Me-Akan in the Akan National Park of Hokkaido.*

the wake of a leader carrying a larger banner. No doubt these banners usually bear no inscription more exciting than the equivalent of 'Detroit Rotary Club' in the United States, or 'Stoke-on-Trent Darby and Joan Club' in England; but the reiteration of the same inscription over and over again, like the exact reduplication of religious or intellectual beliefs, seems to be a potent source of contentment to the Japanese. At many schools all over the world pupils wear uniforms; but only in Japan do all students wear identical black uniforms, with no differentiation other than the crests on their buttons and the badges on their high-necked tunics. All over Japan, the streets, the station platforms and the parks swarm with these black uniforms, each like every other. The girls, too, are uniformed, like sailors who have slipped on navy-blue skirts instead of bell-bottom trousers for a drag-show below decks.

Japan is the most literate nation in Asia, with compulsory education up to the age of fifteen. Fifty per cent of junior high school graduates go to high school; about thirty per cent of high school graduates get to university. There are private universities as well as those run by the Ministry of Education and both have played an important part in the development of modern Japanese education, which—amazingly—did not begin until after 1868.

A university is the key to a job, a good university to a good job. Anyone who does not go to university is doomed to be a second-class citizen for the rest of his days. Since, then, a university education is the *sine qua non* of success in later life, entrance examinations are highly competitive and failure in them leads to despair, disgrace and even suicide. In one university with which I was connected there were 100,000 applicants for 15,000 places in a single year; figures no doubt encouraging to the university in question— since in Japan a staple source of university income is represented by entrance examination fees—but daunting to any would-be student. It is not surprising that, placed under such strain, students in Japan should have embraced the cause of protest with a fanaticism no less hysterical than that with which a former Japanese student generation once marched to war.

The organization of the universities—competition for places apart—is far from satisfactory; the system is old-fashioned and the number of undergraduates (about 50,000 at Nihon University, about 35,000 at Waseda) precludes any close contact between pupil and professor, even in the rare instances when the professor would like such contact to take place. In the classroom, the convention of the professor's infallibility ensures that the students listen to him in passive silence; to question a value judgement, let alone a fact, is to imply that he has no right to be where he is. My seminars in the University in which I was a part-time lecturer tended to be monologues—the response to even the most wilfully provocative of my statements was one of 'If you say it's so, it must be so.' But once out of the lecture-hall or the classroom, the students lose this inbred respect. A venerable scholar of my acquaintance has recently been beaten up for no reason other than that he is Dean of his department; university presidents have been imprisoned by students, with neither food nor drink, for many hours on end; buildings have been torn down and the furniture in them smashed; pitched battles have been fought with the police. Though the main grievances are, naturally, creaky administration and the perpetual rise in fees, politics also play their part; the treaty with the United States that allows for bases in Japan, the continued occupation of Okinawa by American forces and the war in Viet Nam have all received virulent castigation.

Nearer home, cause for discontent springs from the feeling that the ruling Liberal Democratic (*i.e.* Conservative) Party has sacrificed the welfare of the individual to the industrial expansion that has been so amazing a phenomenon of the post-war years. The cost of living rises steeply, year by year; it is difficult to find accommodation. None the less, in spite of their discontents, the middle classes in Japan have tired of the student demonstrations that periodically disrupt all normal life in this or that quarter of this or that city; and the working classes, whose strikes of recent years have been minor and whose processions have been orderly, have also failed to support the cause of student protest in any numbers. The struggle in Japan, as in so many other parts of the world, is not essentially one between classes but between generations.

Even on the young, seemingly so emancipated from the fetters of convention and the past, the Confucian code still exerts an authority of which they are barely conscious. To understand this, it is necessary to understand something of Japan's isolation from the rest of the world for a period of more than two centuries. The Tokugawa Shogunate, which emerged at the beginning of the seventeenth century as the ruling power, defeating all rival feudal lords, brought internal peace to Japan after centuries of civil war. But fearing that contact by feudal lords with foreign powers might bring about its downfall (as it did in the nineteenth century) and also fearing foreign invasion (Spain had occupied the Philippines in 1565), it decided in 1624 to prohibit Spaniards and Portuguese from visiting Japan and all Japanese from travelling overseas. No ocean-going ships were built and anyone who went abroad did so under pain of death should he return. From 1641 the only travellers allowed to visit Japan—and then solely for trading purposes—were the Dutch and the Chinese, and the Dutch were restricted to the small island of Dejima in Nagasaki Bay, now joined to the city of Nagasaki. To isolate Japan in this manner from the rest of the world was not so difficult as it sounds: the nearest point on the mainland is the southern coast of Korea, over a hundred miles across a turbulent sea.

Christian missionaries, who had been in Japan since the arrival of St Francis Xavier in Kagoshima in southern Kyushu in 1549, were now expelled for fear that, as elsewhere in Asia, they might become the agents of colonialism, and were not to return until the Meiji Restoration (1868). Christianity was proscribed and its adherents persecuted. The Tokugawa regime (1615–1868) was entirely secular, ruling the country according to the ethics of Confucius: a code based on obedience, loyalty and the unquestioning performance of duties. The vassal owed loyalty to his overlord, the samurai to his master, the master to the emperor, and these basic loyalties transcended any loyalties to the family: yet within the family, all members owed loyalty to the father, its head. Many young Japanese would vehemently repudiate these tenets, just as many young Europeans would vehemently repudiate the tenets of Christianity; but in both cases a deeply inbred influence remains as an unconscious guide to conduct.

The three main principles of the Confucian code are *ko* (filial piety), *giri* (duty) and *on* (obligation). These duties and obligations run deeper than the gratitude a child feels towards his parents in the West or than the Western cutlet-for-cutlet social ones, and although less rigid today they still play an important part in Japanese life. An *on* (feeling of obligation) was received from the emperor (because he represented Japan), from the parents (because they gave the child life), from the teacher (because he imparted knowledge) and from anyone who performed any service. Today the obligation felt towards the parents, teacher or benefactor is still far stronger than it is in the West. Often when I performed some act of kindness for one of my students he would exclaim with a genuine, not simulated, anguish: 'Mr King, you do too much for me! I cannot repay you!' The pleasure of performing some disinterested favour is often destroyed by the Japanese determination to make a return, at however great a cost. A dinner guest arrives with a bottle of whisky one knows he cannot afford; a student, helped over a thesis, produces an expensive doll. This present-giving in return for favours received has now become such a convention, that gifts, attractively wrapped in coloured paper, are often hoarded unopened (in Japan it is considered ill-bred to open a gift in front of the donor) to be ceded in due course to someone else from whom the recipient has received an *on*.

At every resort or beauty spot, at each of those viewing points on tops of hills or mountains that carry the inscription 'Famous View' or 'Historic View', outside shrines or gardens or temples, there are rows and rows of stalls and little shops selling souvenirs for presents: wooden *kokeshi* dolls, with a waterfall or a tea-house painted on them; gaudy pottery ashtrays; model *torii*. Few Japanese would dream of returning from even a day-excursion without presents for those, family or servants, who have been obliged to stay behind, and many an outing is marred by the worry of deciding what present would be most suitable for Granny and what for the maid. In a department store that is part of Kyoto Station the forgetful traveller, returning home, can buy souvenirs from a variety of regions of Japan, each wrapped as though in the place of its origin.

When, after the downfall of the Tokugawa regime in 1868, Japan entered the modern world, the Confucian code was largely responsible for the astonishing success which attended the processes of Westernization and industrialization. The leaders of the Meiji era had a high sense of duty and patriotism; the people had a respect for authority, springing from a deeply ingrained sense of their *ko*, their *giri*, their *on*. When labour for the new industrial areas was recruited from the countryside, it was disciplined labour, accustomed for generations to strict, feudal rule. The loyalty that a land labourer once owed to his lord was thus transferred to the factory owner. In turn, the employer adopted a paternalistic attitude to his employees and such paternalism is apparent even today, not merely in small companies but in vast international combines. Each worker looks on his firm as his larger family. Employees tend to belong to the same firm for all their working lives; there are factory outings, factory houses for the married, factory dormitories for the unmarried. Once an individual has been accepted by a company, it is highly unusual to dismiss him except for dishonesty or insubordination. Should an unmarried employee have difficulty in finding a wife, the director of his department may well recommend a girl of his acquaintance. Conformity, the terrible conformity of so much Japanese life, is rigorously exacted; and for this reason bachelors are frowned on after a certain age, since they are thought not to have fulfilled the obligation of every man to produce offspring. In many families the eldest son still marries a girl of his father's and mother's choice and subsequently brings her to live in the parental home, where her duty is as much to look after her in-laws as to look after her husband. Girls often refuse to marry an eldest son for fear of becoming no more than a servant of his parents. But wives of eldest sons have one consolation: the grandparents will usually help in the care and education of any children born from the match. In the big towns this old-fashioned form of hierarchal family life is, it is true, already dying out; and in another generation it will probably also be vanishing from the countryside. I have met many husbands, usually among the educated and well-to-do in Tokyo, Osaka, Kobe or Kyoto, who treat their wives more or less as equals, take them to parties and inform them if they are coming home late in the evening; these are things they would never have done formerly.

If, in comparison with that of the Westerner, the day-to-day life of the average Japanese seems hedged in by innumerable prohibitions and demands imposed by convention, there is one area in which the Japanese man enjoys far greater liberty: that of sex. It is, as I have indicated, the primary duty of every Japanese male to marry, produce a family and provide for it; but once that has been performed, the sexual pleasures that he seeks are no one's business but his own—provided of course that in their pursuit he does not ruin himself and so become incapable of supporting his dependants. Well-known figures in business or public life make no secret, though happily married, of keeping mistresses; and if the mistress is a geisha or film-star, then she is a status-symbol as potent as a Rolls Royce or a private plane in the West.

I remember how one well-known Japanese academic in Kyoto would come to my parties in the company now of his dowdy but highly intelligent wife and now of his elegant but bird-brained mistress. Naively, I used to wonder if the wife were aware that she had to take her turn; until at my farewell party, a trio came up my steps—husband in front, and behind, twittering to each other, the two ladies in kimono and *zoki* (formal sandals). In no other country of the world can sexual pleasure, in however bizarre a form, be both so accessible and so little alloyed with fuss, guilt or danger.

I was once present at a meeting between an official of the British Home Office and his counterparts in Japan:

'Now what about the problem of homosexuality?' the British official portentously asked at one point.

'In Japan we have no problem of homosexuality,' the spokesman for the Japanese answered.

'You mean you have no homosexuality?' The British official was incredulous.

'No,' the Japanese corrected him gently. 'I mean that we have no laws prohibiting homosexual conduct.'

In Japan it is no more possible to be a notorious homosexual (or flagellant or exhibitionist or voyeur) than to be a notorious cigar-smoker or beer-drinker or eater of chocolate. Evidence of enjoyment of sex, in all its manifestations, obtrudes wherever one goes, in even the smallest provincial towns; but the Western obsession with sex—so often expressed in privately having it and publicly protesting against others having it—is mercifully absent. None the less, it must be emphasized that Japanese sexual behaviour is always decorous, even in brothels and what are termed 'sister-boy' bars.

Some factories begin their working day with all the workers singing a company song, the burden of which is that the workers must all do their best to make high-grade products for the glory of Japan no less than for the glory of the company. Just as once the sense of discipline infused into the Japanese mind over a period of two hundred years during the Tokugawa regime miraculously facilitated the transition from medieval feudalism to industrialization and urbanization, so now this same sense of discipline, an abiding residue of a past long disowned, is one of the basic reasons for the country's recovery in a period after the Second World War when her entire economic and social structure appeared to be irretrievably in ruins. There are, of course, two other main reasons for this amazing post-war recovery: the enormous aid ($2,000 million, much of which was either food or credit for raw materials) granted by the United States; and the ingenuity, efficiency and forcefulness of management in Japan.

Most Japanese city-dwellers have exiguous quarters. A family that I often visited in Kyoto lived five people to two tiny rooms. Mother, father, son and daughter-in-law all slept in one room; grandfather, who suffered from asthma, slept alone. When a child was born to the young people, I wondered how it could possibly have been conceived in such a total lack of privacy. No doubt because they have to live in such proximity to each other, Japanese have an extraordinary gift for putting up an invisible screen around themselves, behind which they can pursue their private avocations, oblivious to those around them. Often I would visit one of my students in the room he shared with two or three of his fellows. In one corner we would talk together, drink, smoke cigarettes, even eat a meal; in their separate corners his room-mates would continue with their tasks, as though we were invisible and inaudible to them and they to us.

A traditional Japanese room of normal size in a traditional Japanese house of, say, six rooms, is delightful. Its decoration is simple, consisting of just the *tatami* (straw-mats, of a standard size, let into the floor like wood-blocks in parquet), the *shoji* (sliding paper windows) and the *fusuma* (sliding paper doors). The last sometimes have floral designs painted on them, but sparsely—a few irises or peonies, for example.

They are never covered all over with design, like wall-paper in the West. The focal point of the room, corresponding to our hearth, is the raised recess or *tokonoma*, in which the head of the family used to sleep in ancient times. Today the *tokonoma*—unless the room is inhabited by foreign tourists, who often think it a convenient place in which to stack their suitcases—merely contains a scroll picture and a flower-arrangement in a pottery vase. The Japanese regard the Western habit of putting all one's possessions on display as pretentious and vulgar. They change their scroll pictures and their vases regularly with the changes of the season: treasures not on show are kept in the *kura* (if the property is large enough to have one), a store-house with fireproof walls that usually stands in the garden some distance from the house. This same dislike of ostentation leads the Japanese to prefer ornaments of which the colours are subdued: a bowl, for example, of a brown glaze, on which there may be a streak or two of green; or a scroll-picture that is no more than a few black lines on a background wholly white.

The *shoji* (paper windows) can be lifted out of their grooves when the weather is hot, so that the whole of one side of a room is opened to the garden, each spilling into the other and providing the other's complement. In colour a Japanese garden repeats the austerity of the room; showy annuals never appear; instead, there are shrubs, trees and rocks in a pool of raked sand which is surmounted by an ornamental stone bridge.

In contrast to this asceticism of house and garden, the kimono and *obi* (sashes) of young girls are in brilliant, almost jazzy colours. But the traditional clothes of matrons, like those of men, are never bright. Sadly, townswomen now rarely wear kimono in Japan except on social occasions; it is too difficult to cope with the boarding of buses or trains and with hurrying through crowded streets in a costume so constricting.

Modern luxuries such as electric fans, air-conditioning machines, telephones, wirelesses and television sets sometimes ruin the symmetry of a Japanese room, especially when placed in the *tokonoma*. The rooms of otherwise exquisite Japanese inns have been spoiled in this way; but in the best inns of all these adjuncts of modern living are discreetly hidden away, so that the new should not strike a discordant note alongside the old.

When on one occasion I complimented an American professor on the way in which his children had assimilated Japanese manners in his Japanese-style house, he explained: 'I gave them a course of Kabuki to teach them how to behave.' He was right in this: for all the superficial changes in the Japanese home, the customs and manners within it have remained oddly constant for many generations.

The seeds of Kabuki are said to have been sown by Okuni, a dancing-girl at a shrine, who, it is alleged, came to Kyoto at the end of the sixteenth century and performed Buddhist dances and sang religious songs in public. She and a few other women and men acted in farces, adapted from No by her lover, on a simple stage in the dry bed of the River Kamo in Kyoto. In Okuni's troupe men played the parts of women and women played the parts of men; the songs and the plays were distinctly erotic. Then came Women's Kabuki, which was forbidden by the Shogunate in 1629 on the grounds of its immorality—certainly many of its performers were prostitutes. Because of the edict that no women might act, pretty boys took their place, so that Women's Kabuki then became Young Men's Kabuki; but this too was forbidden by the Shogunate, after an unseemly brawl in the theatre, when two samurai fought each other for the favours of a boy-actor. When Kabuki started up again two years later, the parts were played by adult males, who had to hold the audience by acting rather than by deployment of adolescent charm. At the end of the seventeenth century Kabuki had graduated from being a kind of naughty revue to the status of serious theatre. Resident playwrights came into being, stage and scenery were improved, and the musical accompaniment was enhanced by the introduction of the *samisen* (the three-stringed guitar) from South China. The puppet-theatre, with its *joruri* (dramatic ballad) accompaniment, was also developing at this time and some writers wrote for both kinds of theatre.

The word *kabuki* derives from the word *kabuku*, which originally meant 'to incline' but came to mean in the seventeenth century 'to be eccentric', thus carrying with it a hint of the indecent; however, the three ideograms *ka*, *bu*, *ki* mean song, dance and skill (or acting) and they describe exactly the nature of *kabuki*. The singing is not done by the actors, as it is in the Chinese opera, but by members of the orchestra, who may be in the wings, at the side of the stage or at the back of the stage, according to the type of play being performed. The chief instrument is the *samisen*, whose janglingly strident tone is ideal both for accompanying the dramatic ballads (chanted with the most vehement expression of voice and face) and for heightening the tension of a scene with a few plangent notes. The other instruments are flutes, several kinds of drums, cymbals and bells. Wooden clappers are beaten rapidly at the side of the stage to emphasize an entrance or exit or to underline a *mie*—an extraordinary grimace, similar to that to be seen on the faces of guardian statues at the gates of temples.

There are three types of play: *jidaimono*, historical plays dealing with the ruling classes and the samurai; *sewamono*, plays about the lives of ordinary people; and *shosagoto*, dance-plays. A programme usually consists of three or four plays—for example, two *jidaimono*, a *sewamono*, and a dance—and lasts for about five hours. Members of the audience tend to come and go, sometimes even disappearing in search of refreshment in the middle of a scene. The actor usually belongs to a family that has been in Kabuki for generations, being introduced to the audience at the early age of two or three by his father or some other acting member of his family. He can only ascend in his profession by slow degrees, eventually inheriting his father's title on his father's death. No young actor can rocket to stardom on the merits of one successful performance, as in the West.

Although the law forbidding women to appear on the stage was rescinded in the middle of the nineteenth century, there are no actresses in the proper Kabuki theatre even today. Actors play both male and female roles, often during the same play—though it is more usual to specialize in one type of role or the other. An *onnagata*, as the female impersonator is called, is not always successful in a male role, chiefly because his voice tends willy-nilly to rise to the falsetto he has assumed for so many years. One can easily be deceived into believing that an *onnagata* is a woman; indeed, so perfect is an experienced *onnagata*'s general deportment that apprentice geisha are taken to watch him in order to learn how a really well-bred and gracious woman behaves.

Many Kabuki plays are curiously undramatic. They contain effective moments or even half-hours of drama, but tend to trail off from the main plot and lose themselves in complicated sub-plots full of coincidence and mistakes of identity. The famous *Chushingura* (on which John Masefield based *The Faithful*) lasts, with a few acts omitted, for eleven hours; yet we in the West complain of the length of *Parsifal* or *Mourning Becomes Electra*!

The Kabuki stage is large enough to accommodate a complete one-storey Japanese house, with roof and garden at both sides, while at the same time allowing a space between the raised floor of the house and the footlights. The side of the room that faces the audience is naturally open: something usual enough in real life since the paper screens of a Japanese house are often removed in summer. The room, therefore, can be entered from the front, from the main door at the side, or from the back; the garden can be entered either from the *hanamichi* (the 'flower-way'—the raised platform from the rear of the theatre to the stage) or from the wings. Full use is made of all these exits and entrances. At times the stage revolves to reveal the other side of the house and, while it revolves, the actor can walk from room to room. The sets used for historical plays and plays about ordinary people are painstakingly realistic, as is also the acting. For the dance-dramas the simple No-play backdrop of a pine-tree is most common; though on occasion a wisteria-tree may be substituted, its flowers made of paper.

Kabuki is full of conventions which may, at first viewing, strike the Westerner as comic. Fights turn into elaborate ballets; the superman hero will defeat twenty attackers, who somersault about the stage like tumblers; a decapitated enemy will hide his head in his kimono and then run off the stage, as though he were a slaughtered chicken. Kabuki has tender moments but it is often as bloodthirsty as a horror film or Grand Guignol. In one play a geisha murders her madame by first slashing at her with a sword, wounding her dreadfully, and then pushing her into a pond; elated by this butchery, she rushes out to join the revellers in a festival procession that at that moment happens to be passing the house. In another play the heroine is given some medicine by her husband, that causes her terrible disfigurement. In horror, she kills herself; but later returns to haunt her husband as a far from sightly phantom.

Kabuki is pantomime, ballet, opera, comedy, farce and tragedy, often all coexisting within the framework of a single play. A farcical situation may suddenly evolve from a tragic one; moments of superb acting may be interspersed with the broadest of clowning. The audience that attends Kabuki, whether at the Kabuki-za or the new National Theatre, is mostly composed of the middle-aged or old, the majority being women. Almost seventy per cent of any audience is made up of groups of employees whose companies have bought blocks of seats and provincial parties who have come to the capital on sight-seeing trips. Sadly, there is never more than a sprinkling of young people in the theatre. When I used to invite my students to accompany me to Kabuki, they would often confess that they had never until then attended a single performance. Kabuki was too expensive, too slow, they would say; they preferred modern plays, the cinema, television, pop concerts by Japanese groups closely resembling their shaggy Western counterparts, jazz tea-rooms with teenage bands and singers, symphony concerts (there are six symphony orchestras in Tokyo alone), Western-style ballet (there are eighteen companies in Tokyo), and a host of other forms of entertainment. Many of these students, otherwise austere intellectuals, would confess that they spent hours in Pachinko (pin-ball) parlours, mechanically feeding in one silver ball after another, to send it whizzing round the circuit. A Japanese psychiatrist once explained to me, without any hint of humour: 'Masturbation is a substitute for sex and Pachinko is a substitute for masturbation—that is, a substitute for a substitute.'

Five of the six principal shopping and amusement centres of Tokyo are near main-line and suburban railway stations and each pulsates with feverish life. The Japanese, as they often themselves explain, are reserved islanders; but in spite of their shyness, they bring an uninhibited vitality and energy to their quest for pleasure. This energy also manifests itself in the rapidity of their locomotion. People seem to walk more quickly in Tokyo and Osaka than they do in Western cities; trains stop for shorter times at stations; taxis race through the thoroughfares as if they were police-cars in full pursuit of get-away gangs.

The two cardinal events in Japanese recent history were firstly the renunciation by the Emperor of any claims to godhead immediately after the Second World War and secondly the holding of the Olympic

III Fujisan or Fujiyama, Japan's highest mountain (see also ill. 1)

Games in Tokyo in 1964. The first of these events severed the Japanese from their heroically mythical past; the second seemed to promise them a future in which they could take their place in the comity of nations. The opening ceremony of the Games (it included one of the Emperor's rare public speeches) was a remarkable display of Japanese efficiency and powers of organization. The swimming stadium, with its aluminium tent-like roof, designed by Kenzo Tange, most daring and resourceful of modern Japanese architects, was generally acclaimed. Japanese athletes excelled themselves, winning more gold medals than they had ever done before. Most remarkable and most disturbing of all was the victory of the Japanese women's volley-ball team. The members of this team, all employees of the Nichibo cotton-spinning factory, had spent months and months of uninterrupted training, during which all normal human avocations had been sternly renounced. This Japanese singleness of purpose often daunts and repels the foreigner. Students who play in their university or school football or baseball team do virtually nothing else and think of virtually nothing else; amateur actors rehearse eight and nine hours each day, like the most dedicated of professionals.

In recent years the Japanese have frantically embraced sport as though it were a new religion. Professional baseball and Sumo are the most popular of spectator sports; but professional soccer teams have started to appear, no doubt with the World Cup in distant view. There is a keen desire to be supreme in everything: Japan *über Alles*. Golf is popular with senior company executives and prominent citizens on the social make. It is important for a company director to belong to a club where he meets fellow directors, and the deals that were once negotiated in the company of geisha in a tea-house are now often negotiated in the company of female caddies on a green instead. To play golf has become such a status symbol that when I first met the leader of the Tenri sect, he seemed most eager to impress on me not the number of his followers, nor the richness of his sect, nor even the splendour of the university founded in its name, but the fact that he was president of the local golf-club. Chiefly because of the shortage of suitable land and its high rent near cities, it is a very expensive game. If golf is for an élite, ski-ing is for everyone. On winter weekends there is a hectic rush for the ski-ing resorts, trains are jammed with people, inns sleep parties a dozen to a room, and long, patient queues trail away from every slope.

More interesting to the foreigner than any imported sport is Sumo wrestling, said by some authorities to go back to 30 BC. Even if—as seems probable—this is an exaggeration, the sport is certainly an ancient one. At the time of the Meiji Restoration Sumo went into a temporary eclipse, the Japanese authorities fearing that Westerners would deride them for being primitive and uncivilized if they allowed these monstrous giants to manhandle each other in a state of near-nudity. But today Sumo is more popular than ever.

The senior wrestlers weigh up to 350 pounds and, with one or two exceptions, have the pathetic, appealing grotesqueness of pachyderms. With their colossal bellies, their tree-like limbs and their long shining black hair gathered into a top-knot, they are equally astonishing whether seen in kimono strutting or swaying down the street or in nothing but a scanty silk loin-cloth in the ring. Beginning as slim and often handsome youths, they are stuffed, like Strasbourg geese, with a fattening stew called *chankonabe* (made of fish, chicken and pounds of sugar) and with quantities of rice, until they have swollen into the unlovely and obese travesties who enjoy the same kind of popular adoration as tennis-players or football-players in the West.

The wrestlers belong to *heya* (gymnasiums) run by seniors, who may be champions or grand champions. The wrestling itself appears extremely odd to the uninitiated. The actual bout may last only two

IV *Delta landscape on the Nemuro peninsula in eastern Hokkaido.*

seconds and will rarely extend for more than thirty; but the preparatory ritualistic posturings— with the wrestlers spreading wide their arms to show that no weapon is concealed, scattering salt to purify the ring, sipping water to cleanse their mouths, stamping their feet to trample evil into the ground, clapping their hands to frighten evil away, glaring at each other—may last for several minutes. All this elaborate ritual is said to have a close connection with the purification ceremonies of Shinto—a fact that alone indicates the antiquity of the sport. Above the ring there is suspended a roof similar to that of a Shinto shrine and the ring itself is bordered by the same kind of ropes of rice straw as are associated with Shinto.

To the uninitiated it may seem that all that has to be done is for one lumbering human elephant to push another one out of the ring: a tame and boring operation. But in fact there are a vast number of subtle methods of attack, holds and throws that are only perceptible to the expert. Many foreigners attend their first Sumo tournament in a state of hilarity that rapidly turns to boredom; but if one persists in following the fifty-odd senior wrestlers, who fight a bout every day of each of the fifteen-day tournaments and move up and down the proud list according to their performances, one soon turns into an *aficionado*.

Sumo is the cleanest of sports and there is no betting on the wrestlers. The wrestlers themselves often pass the time playing *hanafuda*, a card-game as simple as gin rummy.

There is no large-scale gambling in Japan. True, the machines in the pin-table parlours rattle out their cacophony most of the day and night; but Pachinko is more like hard work than gambling, since many hours must be spent at the machines before a can of fruit or a packet of cigarettes is won. Mahjong is popular, though it has never achieved the ascendancy that it once had in China and still has in Hong Kong. The Japanese play the game quietly, on tables covered with baize or a cloth, and do not crash their tiles down on to bare wood as the Chinese love to do.

Professional gamblers do, however, exist. These curious near-gangsters belong to groups which adhere to an exacting system of loyalties similar to that imposed by the Confucian code. The groups, known as *gumi*, often use construction work as the front behind which they both gamble and intimidate bar owners and night-club proprietors into paying out protection money. Often one can identify a Japanese gangster from the fact that the top joint of his little finger has been amputated in a ceremony of initiation. I ceased to go to one of the biggest night-clubs in Kyoto when one of the girls began to make it her proud habit to circulate among the guests, showing-off a small scent-bottle in which the stump of her current lover's little finger had been pickled in formaldehyde.

To Pachinko, *hanafuda*, Mahjong and, to a small extent, horse-racing must be added a more sophisticated form of gambling—playing the stock market. Security company offices are almost as ubiquitous as betting shops in England, modest numbers of shares being purchasable across the counter as though they were Premium Bonds. Housewives are often to be seen examining the boards on which the latest prices have been quoted—much as they examine the prices outside a supermarket—before scuttling in to take the plunge.

'Did you go to a geisha party?' is probably the most common question put to the tourist returning from Japan. Yet the geisha plays as small a role in the life of the ordinary people of Japan today as the great courtesans of the Third Republic played in the lives of the ordinary people of nineteenth-century France. The West, unaccountably, is fascinated by the geisha. Is she a high-class prostitute? The answer is no: but she does consent to become the mistress of a man of wealth, who will protect her, pay for her expensive wardrobe (one kimono may cost as much as a Balenciaga gown) and, perhaps, when she is getting advanced in years, finance a geisha-house or a shop for her. Geisha-house: like geisha this word, too, carries equivocal overtones for the West, and many times in Kobe drunken foreign sailors would ask me to direct them to the nearest geisha-house, when what they obviously meant was the nearest brothel. So far from being a brothel, a geisha-house is more like a boarding-school. Older geishas run them, looking after their girls like the strictest kind of old-fashioned headmistress, and seeing that they are trained in the arts of the dance, playing the *samisen*, conversation and deportment. Male teachers run exclusive academies of music or the dance to which the apprentice geisha are despatched for lessons. Regularly, twice a year in Tokyo and once a year in Kyoto, the geisha-houses put on displays of their accomplishments for the general public.

Geisha parties are not held in geisha-houses—a misconception common among foreigners—but in the private rooms of Japanese-style restaurants. A glimpse of a geisha on her way from her house to a party is the closest that the Japanese man-in-the-street will usually ever get to one of these costly artificial blooms. Attired in a heavy silk kimono, her dead-white face surmounted by a wig of shiny black hair, the geisha totters along, knock-kneed and shoulders hunched, on special lacquered *geta* or clogs.

The foreigner's first sight of a geisha is exciting; but a quarter of an hour of a geisha party is usually enough. The singing, playing of the *samisen* and the dancing all have their charm; but the mental age of the average geisha seems (it is usually just an affectation, since the majority are highly intelligent) to be that of a girl of twelve. Putting a hand up to cover her teeth, the geisha giggles at your clumsiness with chopsticks. 'King-san,' she simpers in her rudimentary English, 'King-san is handsome boy.' (The compliment becomes meaningless when you hear it repeated to other guests with even less claims to good looks than yourself.) She looks serious and says '*Ah, so des-ka?*' when you produce some platitude. She scrabbles for the silver-wrapping of your cigarette packet and folds it into a crane, which she proudly presents you with. Occasionally she will tell some mildly improper story, making her colleagues squeal with schoolgirl merriment.

A geisha evening is prohibitively costly for anyone not entertaining on an expense account. Expense apart, one wonders how, having experienced this kind of entertainment once or twice, any intelligent man can go on being amused by it for the rest of his days. Yet, inexplicably, such is the case; and companies and even universities are prepared to spend huge sums on geisha parties when entertaining important guests. In the case of company-parties, all the giggling, *samisen*-strumming and *saké*-drinking may finally result in a merger, a take-over or a contract worth several million yen.

Japanese men seem to have a need for a female listener, other than their wives, to whom they can recount their successes or with whom they can discuss their problems. The rich do this with the geisha; the ordinary man with the barmaids, often on the wrong side of forty, who dispense *saké* in the multitude of tiny bars, often seating no more than half-a-dozen customers, that pullulate in even the smallest towns.

One of the most famous scenes in the eighteenth-century Kabuki drama *Chushingura* takes place in the Ichiriki tea-house in Shijo Street in Kyoto. The Ichiriki still stands, looking just as it does on the set of the Kabuki-za. Few foreigners see the inside of the Ichiriki; I only did so because I helped to get the son of a rich Japanese industrialist friend into an Oxford college. To give a party in the Ichiriki, with the highest class of geisha at hand to provide the entertainment, can run away with a mint of money. One sees geisha or *maiko* (apprentice geisha) more frequently in Kyoto than in Tokyo, partly because Kyoto is much smaller and partly because Gion, the main geisha quarter, is right in the heart of the city.

Kyoto is far the most interesting place in Japan and—due to the fact that, unlike other Japanese cities, which sprawl and wind bewilderingly, it was built according to the block-system of the ancient Chinese capital Chang-an—it is also the most convenient. It is bisected by the River Kamo, as Florence is bisected by the Arno, and like Florence, another former capital, it is hemmed-in by hills. Skyscrapers have not yet blocked out the views of these hills from the centre of the city; but ugly modern stores, hotels and apartment blocks have already started to erode the older quarters. Aldous Huxley remarked that Kyoto with its grey wooden houses and grey tiled roofs resembled a Welsh mining village; but this is unfair. True, the houses seem less attractive when looked down upon from the Kyoto tower—a recent monstrosity sited opposite the station; but the narrow lanes of quarters like Gion or Niomon-dori are enchanting, with none of the 'Olde Worlde' atmosphere that has been diligently preserved at some Western historic sites. The inhabitants live as their parents and grandparents lived. The alleys are too narrow for motor-cars but not for the bean-curd man's bicycle, the kimonoed lady with her open, gaily-coloured parasol or for the rats that, even in broad daylight, can often be seen scavenging in the gutters. The public bath-house is regularly patronized and remains the 'club' of the quarter. Once a year, on a day in August, each street of this sort has its *o-soji* (honourable cleaning) when the women remove their sliding windows and doors and take up their *tatami* mats, leaning them against the outside of the houses and then vigorously beating them. It is a day of commotion, disruption and dust; but by evening it is all over and the doors and windows are back in place and the *tatami* relaid.

Japanese are always proclaiming that Tokyo is best for Kabuki, Kyoto for No and Osaka for Bunraku (puppet-theatre). The last is a moribund art, barely kept alive by television, cabaret performances and foreign tours. It is sad to see skilled puppeteers, often old men who have devoted their lives to the art, in the alien and unsuitable surroundings of a night-club. There is much to be admired in Bunraku. Chikamatsu Monzaemon (1653–1724), often called 'The Shakespeare of Japan', preferred writing for the puppet-theatre to writing for Kabuki, because in the former there were no actors to argue about interpretation or to insist on larger parts. Gordon Craig would have sympathized with this viewpoint. Now, however, many plays originally written for puppets have been assimilated into the Kabuki repertoire, many of the actors' traditional movements, gestures and expressions being based on those of the puppets.

One can see No performances in Tokyo and Osaka; but this really great theatre is at its best in Kyoto, the ancient capital. Not far from the Niomon-dori, a quarter old-fashioned enough to hold an annual *o-soji*, and near the Heian Shrine, is the Kanzé Kaikan No theatre. Kanzé is one of the five schools of No. Each school differs slightly (not noticeably to the tiro) in the way the lines are spoken and the play presented. No is very much a relic of the past, having been preserved from the fourteenth century in almost exactly the same form as we see it today. There have, it is true, been attempts to write modern No plays, notably by Yukio Mishima, the famous novelist and playwright; but these do not count as proper No, which has in its repertoire some 240 plays, all at least 450 years old. Kan-ami (1333–84), the founder of the Kanzé school, and his son Ze-ami (1363–1443), both superb writers, actors and musicians, were the men most responsible for the development of No.

No has often been compared to Greek classical drama: both have choruses, the principal actors are masked and the themes are usually tragic. There are no women players in No—men take women's parts,

V *Conifers and moss on the eastern slope of the Daisetsu mountains in the north of the Daisetsuzan National Park on Hokkaido.*

VI *(Overleaf) A group of pilgrims of the Nichiren sect on a visit to the temple on Koyasan, which was founded in 816 by Kobo-Daishi as the centre of the Shingon sect and has been frequently restored since then.*

as in Kabuki—and the plots of most of the dramas can be summed up in half-a-dozen lines. For example, in *Shunkan* by Ze-ami, three men have been exiled on a desolate island for plotting against the ruling Heike family. A messenger arrives with a pardon, but only for two of them, so that Shunkan, the third, must remain behind, wistfully watching as his companions sail away to the capital. That is all, a tiny theme; but it is given a remarkable resonance by the hieratic movements of the actors and by a music, all thumps, rattles, moans and sudden glissandos, produced by a small orchestra—flute, two hand-drums, occasionally a stick-drum and a male chorus. The language, in a medieval Japanese incomprehensible to all but serious scholars of No, is allusive and symbolic; the acting and delivery wholly stylized.

The slow-motion walk of the No actor is based on that of the Zen priest; and the austerity of this art is similar to that of other Japanese arts derived from Zen Buddhism—the tea-ceremony, black-ink landscape-painting *(sumie)*, pottery, flower-arrangement and landscape gardening. It is due to the influence of Zen, with its emphasis on the need for unity with nature, that the Japanese delight in restraint in art. (Their word for such restraint, *shibui*, has already found its way into the glossy magazines of the West.) An unglazed pot from Bizen, bearing faint irregular markings due to iron in the clay, would be *shibui*; a gorgeous kimono would not be, any more than a brilliant abstract painting.

Zen monasteries still function and attract visitors, both because many of them possess exquisite gardens and works of art and because they offer a regime of disciplined meditation. Anyone may join a monastery for a time without becoming a postulant: at liberty to sit in the hall of meditation with the resident monks and so to attempt to reach *satori* (enlightenment). Zen, emanating from China, was one of the four new sects that arose in the thirteenth century, a period when Buddhism had become corrupt. Its main doctrines are 'Look carefully within and there you will find the Buddha' and 'Seek salvation by meditation and divine emptiness'. With its metaphysical approach, its *koan* or riddles (the best known of which is the question 'What is the sound of one hand clapping?') and its rigid discipline, Zen, like No, was never meant for everybody and attracted only the aristocrats and the samurai. The insistence of the Zen philosophy on the unimportance of physical hardship particularly appealed to the warrior class. Zen's emphasis on self-restraint and asceticism produced in art black-ink landscape painting (the best Japanese examples of this style of painting are by Sesshu, 1420–1506); calligraphic scroll pictures, the execution of which may take only a few seconds after a lifetime of laborious practice; earthenware pots glazed in monochrome or sombre hues; flower-arrangements *(ikebana)* consisting of no more than three blooms, a branch and a leaf or two; landscape gardens, the most austerely effective of which, like Soami's famous garden at Ryoanji in Kyoto, are made up of a few rocks scattered over a space of raked white gravel; and the tea-ceremony.

One might say that the tea-ceremony is the pivot of all these various branches of art, for the tea-house, itself modelled on the hut of a renowned Zen priest, is set in a garden; the four-and-a-half-mat room in which the tea is served is decorated with a scroll-picture and a flower-arrangement; and the handleless cups, often of great value, are made of pottery. The tea-ceremony became popular among the samurai in the Muromachi age (1339–1573), a period of unremitting violence and civil war. Such a peaceful and strictly formal function acted as a needed antidote to the turmoil and conflict of the warrior's life.

The ceremony is carried out according to rules which the tea-master and his five guests must follow rigidly in all particulars; even the admiring by the guests of the cups and utensils used in the making of the tea—tea-caddy, bamboo spoon, bamboo-whisk for stirring the emerald tea-powder—must be carried out

VII Passing through a series of red-painted torii the visitor enters the Inari Shrine in the Fushimi suburb of Kyoto.

not spontaneously but according to a ritual. Often, after attending the tea-ceremony, one of the Japanese participants would whisper to me as we left: 'Fancy a man so rich using such ugly cups'; but the cups would have been admired none the less, carefully fondled, praised for their shape and shade. Although religion is not conspicuously involved, the tea-ceremony is akin to a religious ceremony: both an exercise in self-discipline and an aid to contemplation of the infinite and to communion with nature.

The love of nature is strong in the Japanese and the Japanese are more aware of the seasons than we in the West. Scroll pictures, women's kimono and flower-arrangements all vary according to the time of the year; and in the *haiku* (a poem of seventeen syllables) there must be one word which denotes what season it is.

The gardens of the temples in Kyoto are among the most beautiful in the world, once one has accepted the conventions of the enclosed formal garden. Visitors from other countries, however, find it difficult to do this: one such was Vita Sackville-West, who expressed horror at trees, shrubs and flowers being 'wilfully tortured', as she put it. But whether it be the esoteric rock-garden of Ryoanji, or the moss-garden of Kokedera, or the ingenious garden of the Katsura palace, the masterpiece of the Japanese Capability Brown, Kobori Enshu (1579–1647), or the several gardens of the various sub-temples of Daitokuji, all of the gardens in and around Kyoto seem to me incomparable in their beauty and tranquillity. Occasionally, it is true, there is some of that Barrie-type whimsy so dear to the Japanese. For example, the garden of Konchi-in, a subsidiary of Nanzenji, is called the Crane and Turtle garden because it contains two stunted pines, one of which has been made to grow into a shape that is supposed to represent a crane, the other a turtle; but one would never guess this unless one was told it. Japanese often see such similarities where none exists to Western eyes. Lake Biwa near Kyoto is called after the musical instrument of that name. The lake has eight views—to my eyes no more beautiful than many other views from around its shores— which have been specially selected and given names like 'Flight of Wild Geese at Katata', 'Night Rain at Karasaki', 'Sunshine with a Breeze at Awazu', 'Evening Glow at Seta', 'Sails Returning at Yabase'. Even when there are no geese at Katata, no rain at Karasaki, no sunshine or breeze at Awazu, no evening glow at Seta and no sails at Yabase, Japanese tourists still bundle out of their cars at each of these acknowledged beauty-spots in turn, to click their cameras and to exclaim their appreciation.

It has often been said that the Japanese have the enviable ability to see only what they want to see or ought to see, and that this explains their apparent indifference to ugliness rearing up alongside beauty. They do not notice, as we do, the dead branch on the cherry-tree, the litter at the beauty-spot, the shirt on a hanger in the living-room; these things *should* not be there, therefore they *are* not there. So much more sensitive than ours in so many respects, Japanese eyes can none the less be trained to ignore things like a ferro-concrete hotel on top of a mountain; the network of wires that dangles, like some giant cobweb, over an exquisite temple; the shoebox buildings dotted here and there in a street otherwise lined with small, elegant wooden houses; the factory on the slope of Mount Fuji. Western eyes also, of course, have to accustom themselves to the spoiling of the towns and countryside by tasteless, discordant, shoddy buildings; but they are less able to do so than Japanese ones.

This ability to overlook the ugly and distasteful enters into social life as well. It is not, for example, considered polite to use the word *ee-e* (No) in conversation, since to refuse a request bluntly is something a Japanese finds irksome. The smile a shop-assistant gives as he or she utters the word *arimasen* ('We haven't any') is meant, not to show perverse delight at balking the would-be purchaser but to mitigate the bad news. When I announced to a group of my students that one of my dogs had died in great agony after being poisoned by a heartless burglar, I was furious at their apparent callousness in going off into gales of laughter. But a Japanese friend later explained to me that this laughter was the laughter of acute embarrassment. If one of them had been telling me of the death in similar circumstances of his own dog, or even of a friend or relative, he would also have laughed, in an attempt to minimize the loss and so save me from pain.

A direct request in Japan is considered gauche and self-praise unmannerly. A host will apologize for the inadequacy of his hospitality even when it has been lavish; he may even—as one rich Osaka industrialist did with me—go to the length of denigrating his possessions and referring to his wife as an ugly, incapable old bag. Of course he does not really mean this or wish you to think that he means it: he is merely following convention. Often, after one has taken a Japanese out on an excursion, he says to one, 'Please excuse me, I am afraid that I have behaved very badly,' when in fact his conduct and demeanour have both been beyond reproach. Such a declaration astonishes the foreigner, who does not realize that it is merely a polite formality. Modesty is admired in Japan, boasting abhorred; but this does not mean that all Japanese are modest or that none of them discovers subtle means of boasting. Foreigners often find that the Japanese's ostentatious modesty gets on their nerves: especially when, for example, a Japanese, having claimed to be a hopeless player of golf, tennis or bridge, then turns out to be an expert. Before a bout a Sumo wrestler does not prance around the ring, braggishly acknowledging the cheers of his fans; instead, with solemn face, he goes through the prescribed ritualistic preliminaries. In victory, he shows no sign of triumph; in defeat, no trace of disappointment. At the end of the No play the actors slowly leave the stage, as though deaf to all applause; in Kabuki the players never take curtain calls.

There is a bewildering difference between Japanese manners in private and Japanese manners in public. At home a Japanese is scrupulously polite to a guest, behaving with total self-effacement and almost going beyond what is expected of a host: he invites the guest to bath first in the family tub, to sit in the place of honour with his back to the *tokonoma*, to sleep in the best room; and if the guest is a foreigner, the Japanese host may even go to the trouble and expense of providing Western food, which he himself may hate. Yet beyond the *tatami* of his own home a Japanese often behaves thoughtlessly and even boorishly, pushing in a me-first way on to buses and trams, making audible personal remarks about strangers, staring and giggling. When I had a bad fall down some steps in Tokyo, it was some time before a good Samaritan—a Korean garbage-collector—came to my aid. On another occasion, driving from Kobe to Kyoto, I saw a truck swerve off the road and crash into a paddy-field. The four cars ahead of me merely drove on; it was my driver and I who stopped and rushed to the rescue. This lack of public spirit or even of simple humanity is explained by the twin Japanese fears of taking on an extra responsibility in a life already overburdened with responsibilities and of putting a stranger under an obligation. When an American friend of mine saved a young girl who was trying to commit suicide by drowning, he was scarcely dry before it had been made clear to him that, having interfered outside his own circle, he was now responsible for the girl's future in the months ahead.

Ruth Benedict in her admirable book *The Chrysanthemum and the Sword* says that the Japanese people belong to a 'shame culture', whereas we of the West belong to a 'guilt culture'. People of a shame culture live in fear of bringing shame or loss of face on themselves, their family or their country, by acting in a way that might cause outside people to deride them; people of a guilt culture live in fear of what their own consciences will tell them if they do wrong. Most Japanese live in exaggerated fear of what others will think; to get on in one's career, it is necessary to conform to a narrow path long since laid out for one.

It is a terrible solecism in Japan to cause anyone a loss of face; but it is one that Westerners are always unwittingly committing. One should not, for example—as I eventually learned—ask a student if he has passed an examination because, should he have failed, the question will cause pain; one should either wait until the information is offered voluntarily or elicit it in a devious manner. Similarly, in class, if one wishes to criticize the behaviour or the work of a student, it is essential to do so privately after the period is over and not before his fellows. Admired behaviour is that which shows deep consideration for the feelings of others.

Understatement, ellipses, guarded hints form the basis of the Japanese approach to social intercourse. It is true, of course, that such an approach is common to the whole of the Orient and not confined to Japan alone: but Japan, superficially so much more Westernized than, say, India or Thailand, demonstrates it in a more extreme form than any other nation of the East today.

'Isn't Japan all Americanized now?' a Westerner will ask. Yes, outwardly much of it is; but though Japan has adopted Western technical discoveries and has even improved on some of them—the camera and the transistor-radio, for instance—though she has adapted Western ways of living, grafting armchairs, desks, dining-tables and beds on to Japanese rooms, and though she has adopted Western food in a number of her hotels and restaurants, yet she has not basically altered her character. A Japanese in a Western suit or dress is no less Japanese than one in a kimono; nor does a Japanese by eating steak and salad make himself un-oriental.

When foreign ideas and techniques are introduced into a country they are often changed, adapted and extended if that country already has a strong national identity of its own. This is what has happened in Japan, not merely in the fields of science, economics and medicine, but also in that of culture. Japanese artists—like those of the Gutai Group, for example—would be the first to acknowledge that they owe a great debt to painters like Jackson Pollock, Ben Nicholson and Mondrian; yet the best of them produce pictures that are as inescapably Japanese as Van Gogh's adaptation in oils of Hiroshige's wood-block print 'Sudden Shower at Ohashi' (1857) is inescapably European.

Lady Murasaki, that astonishing genius who, in *The Tale of Genji*, gave the world its first novel, was of course uninfluenced by the West; but from the late nineteenth century Japanese writers have owed a huge debt first to Europe and now, in recent years, also to America. The late Akutagawa Rynosuke, author of bitter, Swiftian satires on society, the most famous of which was '*Kappa*', had read Kafka; Soseki was an admirer of Jane Austen; and the work of the late Junichiro Tanizaki, Yasunari Kawabata (1968 Nobel Prize Winner), and the popular novelist Yukio Mishima would not be the same had Western literature (especially Dostoievsky, Proust, Joyce, Lawrence and Faulkner) remained unknown to them.

Meat was not eaten in Japan before the mid-nineteenth century, when the period of isolation, lasting almost two hundred and fifty years, ended and foreigners were allowed into the country again. Being Buddhist, the Japanese were vegetarian; though, curiously, they had always been fish-eaters, since fish,

VIII *The principal image in the Byodo-in Temple at Uji near Kyoto is the representation of the Buddha Amitabha in gilded wood, a masterpiece of Fujiwara art carved by Jocho in 1053. Amida is represented sitting on a lotus flower in the classic attitude of meditation. The statue is 8 ft 6 in. high.*

 IX *The Phoenix Hall (ho-o-do) of the Byodo-in Temple at Uji near Kyoto. The regent Fujiwara-no-Michinaga (966–1024) had built himself a country seat here; it was extended in 1052 to become a Buddhist monastery, which belongs to the Amida-Nyorai school.*

fowl and rabbits—the last falling into the category of birds—were exempt from prohibition. Today raw fish, especially tuna (maguro) and sea bream (tai) are delicacies. Raw tuna fish and sea bream are luxury foods and are not by any means eaten every day or even once a week in the ordinary middle-class household. Most families also now include Western dishes in their bill of fare. In the 1860's, butchers' shops began to open for foreigners, and some advanced Japanese even at that early date took to the eating of pork and beef, claiming that to do so improved both physique and brain. However, it was not until the Allied occupation after the Second World War that the man-in-the-street took to eating meat, bread, butter and processed cheese and to drinking milk. Although there is no proof for the commonly made claim that this new diet has made the Japanese more intelligent (they have always been that), it is obvious to anyone who travels in the subway in Japan that it has made them taller: the young stand head-and-shoulders above the old.

Just as in the ricefields round an up-to-date factory men and women, wearing primitive straw-hats, work knee-deep in mud, so ancient festivals, both Buddhist and Shinto, continue to survive in this highly industrialized and materialistic society. One of the most extraordinary of these festivals is that held at Konomiya near Nagoya, the Coventry or the Detroit of Japan. It is known as the Naked Festival (hadaka matsuri) and, though Shinto itself, has a Buddhist counterpart at Saidaiji near Okayama. A villager is chosen to be the God-man (Shingotoko), and a week before the festival he goes to live in the shrine for purification purposes. On the day of the festival he is dressed in priestly robes, sits in the shrine and receives homage from the villagers. He then changes into nothing but a loin-cloth and slips into an enclosure that is seething with men and youths (perhaps as many as 5,000) similarly garbed. The idea is that as many people as possible should touch the God-man, since by so doing they pass their bad luck and evil into him. After fighting his way through the mass of roaring, sweating, struggling bodies, he returns to the shrine. In the middle of the night he passes the bad luck and evil into a rice-cake, which he buries outside the village. The sides of the arena (actually the main roadway to the entrance to the shrine) are lined with stands that become jammed with spectators, many of them with cameras. After the ceremony is over, the participants quickly recover from a frenzy exaggerated by a liberal consumption of beer and saké, don their trousers, shirts, jackets and overcoats and then soberly make their way home, as though returning from a quiet picnic in the country. The next day sees them at their desks, behind their counters, tending their machines, or whatever is their daily occupation.

At the O-Bon festival (a sort of Buddhist equivalent of All Souls' Day) at Tokushima on the island of Shikoku, the whole town rocks in dance and throbs with drum-beats for three nights of August. The Dance is called the Awa-odori, a measure of simple steps performed by groups in line. Today, however, there has been modernization to the extent that rival groups, drawn from factories or companies in the surrounding district, compete for prizes.

At Sendai there is the Star Festival, when the streets are lined with tall bamboo branches decorated with baubles and streamers; in Kyoto there is the week-long Gion festival, with the creation of a Sacred Page and the dragging of huge shrine-floats and palanquins through the streets by men in loin-cloths and jacket-length kimono (happi coats); at Sapporo there is the Winter Festival during which giant effigies are fashioned from snow. There are innumerable other festivals all over the country—at least one for each day of the year: some are connected with the ploughing of the rice-fields or the transplanting of the young rice-shoots, others with fishing. The agricultural festivals are lengthy and fascinating, with brilliantly coloured traditional costumes and music and songs.

Since so many of these festivals are rich in entertainment, the prying eye of the television camera is now often present when they are celebrated, even in the most remote areas of the country. Such publicity destroys spontaneity and gives the villagers the illusory notion that vast sums of money can be made. Remove folk festivals from their original setting and put them on the television screen or stage (a Tokyo ballet company has performed the Deer Dance from northern Honshu) and they at once become emasculated, their real meaning getting confused with the demands of commercial entertainment. At a rice-transplanting ceremony which I attended at a festival near Osaka, the girls who carried the sheaves of rice wore magnificent kimono and headgear and more than one had the toenails of her naked feet painted crimson. They looked more like show-girls than country lasses; perhaps they were.

Westerners often ask if Japanese people can read Chinese writing. The answer is that they can. They are able to get the gist of an article in a Chinese newspaper, for Japanese, although a totally different language from Chinese, is written with Chinese characters and part of its vocabulary was borrowed from China in the same way that the English language adopted Latin and Greek words. Japanese is polysyllabic while Chinese is tonal, and as well as ideograms Japanese is written with the aid of two syllabaries (each of 48 sounds)—*kata-kana* and *hira-gana*—which are tacked-on to, or mixed-up with, the Chinese characters. Both syllabaries are old (eighth century AD), but today *kata-kana* is employed for the writing of foreign names and telegrams and *hira-gana* for indicating verbal inflections and for writing postpositions and conjunctions. It is perfectly possible to write Japanese in *hira-gana* (Lady Murasaki wrote the whole of the *Tale of Genji* in it, since women were forbidden to use the supposedly more noble ideogram in her day) and people do in fact often use this syllabary for the writing of letters, since, unlike ideograms, it can be written cursively. On the occasions when ideograms are ambiguous (they can have several meanings), *hira-gana* signs are put underneath them—on station platforms, for example, where any ambiguity might be disastrous to the traveller. Because of the ambiguity of the ideogram it is sometimes difficult for a name to be read on the visiting cards that all Japanese carry around with them as though fearful of losing their identities. This problem is overcome by the owner of the card saying his name aloud as he presents it.

Japanese is not difficult to pronounce and, when spoken, resembles Italian. A few years ago I attended a performance of *Aida* in which the tenor sang in Italian and the soprano in Japanese, without the incongruity seeming laughable. Japanese is a language in which unequivocal statements are often hard, and it is therefore suited to a people who shrink from being totally unequivocal. Frequently, when I would ask my secretary to telephone for me in Japanese a message of a single sentence, it would then take him five minutes to do so. Partly no doubt this was due to the Japanese convention of hurry being impolite; but partly it was due to the difficulty of making a statement that did not admit of a number of different interpretations. One of the oddities of Japanese is the way in which numeration varies according to the nature of things to be counted. There are about thirty different ways of counting but fortunately now only eight in general use, and these depend on whether one is counting people, animals, birds, books, round things, long things, flat things or cupfuls of liquid. Honorifics are obligatory. The suffix *san* is attached to a person's name and the prefix *O* to a noun, so that one talks, for example, of *Tanaka-san* (Tanaka-honourable) and *O-sake* (honourable *saké*). When I first went to Japan, I used unwittingly to cause mirth by asking for 'O-benjo' (the honourable lavatory).

Foreigners who go to the trouble of learning the language usually find that their Japanese friends, so far from being flattered, seem on the contrary vaguely resentful and disapproving. This is probably because Japanese take a pride in their reputation for being unfathomable and unpredictable and fear that anyone who can talk to them in their own language may soon find out that, for the most part, they are sphinxes without a secret. Certainly there is no country in the world in which the people are less willing to instruct the foreigner about national customs and institutions.

From time to time, even as early as at the beginning of this century, there have been Japanese who have urged the abandonment of the ideogram in favour either of *hira-gana* or Roman letters. The sight of a Japanese typewriter is the most potent of arguments in favour of such reform. But however beneficial to commerce, the disappearance of Chinese characters would cause a great loss to poetry and the art of calligraphy. In the *tanka* (poem of 31 syllables) and the *haiku* (17 syllables), it is not merely the sound and meaning of each ideogram that is important; no less important is its shape and the juxtaposition of that particular shape to the shapes around it. Black and white *(sumie)* paintings are executed with the same brush that is used for writing ideograms—an indication of how much more closely related are poetry and painting in Japan and China than in the West. Even the common neon sign urging one to drink a patent preparation designed to extend one's virility has an exotic beauty until the moment when one learns to read what it actually says.

If ever I wanted to evoke a certain laugh from my students, all I had to do was to mispronounce a few words in Japanese. If the mispronunciation also happened to produce a pun, a play on words in which the Japanese delight, the class would be convulsed with mirth. There was, for example, a Miss Hidaka and, on one occasion, by mistake I called her Miss Hadaka (Miss Naked): the laughter went on for minutes.

A sophisticated Westerner finds Japanese humour puerile and feels that his jokes usually cause laughter only because his listeners know that they are meant to be funny and laugh out of either politeness or a sense of duty. When William Faulkner was lecturing with the aid of an interpreter in Japan, he told a long and rambling joke, which the interpreter appeared to translate in about thirty seconds flat, causing the audience to rock with laughter and even applaud. When the lecture was over, the puzzled and admiring Faulkner asked the interpreter how he had managed to get across the point of the story with such brevity and to such effect. 'Oh, Mr Faulkner, please forgive me,' the interpreter replied. 'Your story was too difficult for me to follow. So I just said, "Mr Faulkner has told us an extremely funny joke".'

There is much *schadenfreude*—for which, like the Germans, the Japanese have a pronounced taste—in the slapstick of Japanese television or film comics; and this same *schadenfreude* is an important element in the naive humour of the *kyogen* or traditional farces that are performed between No plays and are as old as No itself. In short, one cannot say that the Japanese are a humorous, much less a witty, people; or that they have in any marked degree the ability to laugh at themselves. There are exceptions, of course, to this generality; but these exceptions usually belong to a group of people who have been deeply influenced by the West. The best advice to anyone who wishes to make his Japanese hosts laugh is to forget about the witticisms and to contrive, instead, either to fall flat on his face or to sit on a chair that is not there.

It is possible that the constant earth-tremors in the capital contribute to the hectic vitality one notices as soon as one sets foot there: catastrophe came to Tokyo and Yokohama in 1923 and no resident of Tokyo can ever entirely banish from his mind the thought that it might recur in a even more violent form. The law forbidding the erection of tall buildings was rescinded in 1963, when allegedly earthquake-proof houses began to go up; but the experience of Niigata in 1964, when in a fairly strong earthquake whole modern apartment blocks leaned over at perilous angles, is hardly encouraging.

Japan is a country of endless natural catastrophes; and it may be because of these that the Japanese are a people so absorbed in thoughts of death. Typhoons are a constant danger, particularly at the time of the autumn equinox. Spawned in the Pacific, they snake their uncertain way up to Japan or along the coast of China. In my first typhoon, an Australian guest and I decided that the Japanese, who had left the streets totally deserted, were making an unnecessary fuss about a triviality, and decided to venture out. When sheets of corrugated iron off neighbouring roofs began to whizz horizontally across the streets and we were in imminent danger of being decapitated, we ignominiously rushed into a public lavatory. Floods and fires are other hazards so common that scarcely a year passes without hundreds of people losing all their possessions and even their lives in one or the other. Having experienced a fire in Kyoto—an overturned stove in one wooden house had in a few minutes ignited all those around it and ringed the office in which I was working with flames—I readily understand why every town and many villages in Japan contain look-out towers, from which watch can be kept.

The first delight that Japan offers is an aesthetic one: essentially, her culture derives from the senses rather than the intellect and over the centuries the Japanese have developed an aesthetic sensibility far in advance of any nation of the Western world. The humblest meal in the humblest inn is presented as though it were a work of art—the colours of the various vegetables fastidiously offsetting each other, the vegetables themselves carefully sculpted; the humblest cup or plate or towel is impeccable in the grace and simplicity of its traditional design; even the matchboxes are small works of art. There is much that is hideous in many an over-all view—gigantic hoardings, sagging overhead telephone wires, concrete apartment-blocks—but take each view apart and most of its components, from dwarf shrubs to wooden fences, to half-length curtains above the doors of shops, will be seen to be models of restrained, unselfconscious and careful artistry. On one occasion when I was motoring with a much-travelled Greek friend along the untarred roads to the east of Matsue, he suddenly and unaccountably fell silent and glum. 'What's the matter?' I asked at last. 'All these years,' he replied, 'I've been thinking that Greece is the most beautiful country in the world, and now I know that it is not.' One can see his point: Japan probably *is* the most beautiful country in the world, even though whole areas of it are of an unparalleled hideousness.

Whether it is possible to lose one's heart to the people of Japan, as it is only too easy to do to the country, is debatable. With their reserve, their quiet self-esteem, their often ruthless efficiency, their over-sensitive regard for the feelings of friends which coexists with an almost total disregard for the sufferings of strangers or of animals, their lack of spontaneity, their belief in duty and self-discipline and abnegation, the Japanese are—in contradistinction to the Greeks—admirable but not lovable. Certainly they stimulate anyone who comes into contact with them, being full of confidence in themselves and in the future. The goals are there, there is little dispute about them; and with a remarkable cohesion, in spite of all superficial differences of political opinion, the Japanese are sweeping towards these targets like a conquering army on the march. It is remarkable that after the traumatic events of Hiroshima, the Emperor's renunciation of divinity, and the American occupation, any nation should be so totally and so unheedingly sure of its destiny.

My special thanks are due to John Haylock who, throughout the writing of this essay, has generously given me the full benefit of his wider and deeper knowledge of Japan.

FRANCIS KING

The Discovery of Japan

'Zipangu is an island in the eastern ocean. It is of considerable size.

'The inhabitants have fair complexions, are well made and civilized in their manners. Their religion is the worship of idols and independent of every foreign power.' With these words the Venetian, Marco Polo, gave his fellow Europeans the first description of the Land of the Rising Sun in the year 1298. Reports by subsequent and better-informed travellers did not bear out his account of the fabulous supplies of gold in this remote country, still less his grotesque assertion that prisoners who could not find the money to buy their freedom were roasted alive on a spit—'and they say that human flesh surpasses every other in the excellence of its flavour'.

The Portuguese seafarers in the 16th century, who produced more accurate reports on the islands of the Far East, were also impressed by the civilized customs of the people, and St Francis Xavier, who worked as a missionary in Japan from 1549 to 1559, wrote: 'The people with whom we came in contact excel in piety all other peoples since discovered, so that I believe there is no barbarian nation which can compare with the Japanese for natural goodness. They have an alert and open mind and are very concerned with honour and reputation. Honour they esteem above all else. While many of them are poor, poverty is held to be no disgrace. They are very polite among themselves. The majority can read and write. They are by nature very proper in their behaviour and have extremely enquiring minds.'

The first detailed report on Japan was by a doctor, Engelbert Kämpfer, from Lemgo. He went to Kyushu towards the end of the 17th century as a member of a Dutch trade mission and was received by the shogun in Edo. This was his general impression:

'Japan—Nippon or Land of the Rising Sun to the natives—is the name of the island, of which Europeans first learned from Marco Polo who called it Zipangu, a world of unknown origin. But this realm consists not of one island but of several, which, like Great Britain, are separated from each other by many narrow sea-channels and lie in the most remote Orient. Nature has surrounded this realm with an impregnable protective wall and has thereby made it invincible, as it is surrounded on all sides by a sea that is hostile to seafarers . . .

'The inhabitants have no lack of boldness, or should I call it bravery? With a noble contempt for life and with stoical courage they do not shrink from laying hand upon themselves, should they be overcome by enemies or incapable of avenging some shame inflicted on them. When one reads the history of their civil wars, one cannot but admire the signal boldness with which they have demonstrated their courage against one another in previous centuries.'

The Encyclopédie of Diderot and D'Alembert, which appeared in 1757, also expressed its admiration for the forceful character of this people in their astonishingly self-contained world and pointed out in particular that, while Japan and China might appear to have much in common, there were certain fundamental differences:

'The weather in this great country is very uncertain. In winter it can be bitterly cold, in summer, on the other hand, extremely hot. There is much rain throughout the entire year, more especially in the months of June and July, but without the periodical regularity that is characteristic of the warmer areas of eastern India. Lightning and thunder are frequent. The sea that surrounds Japan is very stormy, and shipping is endangered by the large number of rocks and by the shallows and reefs above and below the water.

'The country is for the most part mountainous, stony and arid; but the industry and tireless activity of the inhabitants, who are moreover extremely abstemious, have made it productive and independent of the neighbouring countries. The entire people lives on rice, vegetables and fruit; its sobriety is a token of virtue rather than of superstition. There is no shortage of sweet water, as there are many lakes, rivers and both cold and warm, mineral-rich springs. Not infrequently there are earthquakes, which with their violent, protracted shocks sometimes destroy whole towns.

'While Japan has captured the interest of geographers, it merits possibly even more the interest of philosophers. This astonishing people is the only one in Asia that has never been conquered and appears to be unconquerable ... Japan is reminiscent of England for its insular pride and for the suicide which is believed to be a frequent occurrence at both these extremities of our hemisphere ...

'Japan is no less densely populated or less active than China but as a nation is more proud and courageous. It possesses everything we lack. The peoples of the Orient were at one time remarkably superior to us in the West in all the arts and crafts. But we have made up for lost time, Monsieur de Voltaire adds! Today the Oriental peoples are no more than barbarians or children in the fine arts, despite their antiquity and all that they owe to nature ...'

One can see that these Frenchmen of the Enlightenment were already familiar with the two widely divergent views of Japan which were subsequently put forward: respect for an ancient culture, and the frequently blind arrogance of the 'civilized'. Among the latter is Pierre Loti, author of *Madame Chrysanthème*, who wrote of Japan at the time of the Meiji reforms: 'I find it small and antiquated, bloodless and lacking in vitality; I am aware of its antediluvian antiquity, of its centuries-old mummification, which, in contact with western evolution, will soon degenerate into something grotesque and comic.'

And here finally, to round off the image of this remote island people which had been built up in the West, is how the Meyer *Conversationslexicon* of 1850 summed up the Japanese national character:

'Opinions of the character of the people are mostly favourable. Anxiety to learn, cunning, humour, shrewdness, diligence, courage, moderation, politeness, frugality, cleanliness almost to a fault, love of justice, honesty and, in particular, a high sense of honour are registered on the credit side of their character, pride, a lust for revenge (blood-feuds were common), cruelty, duplicity and, in particular, superstition and a craving for the creature comforts, on the debit side. As a result of their exaggerated sense of honour duels are a very frequent occurrence among the Japanese, and a peculiar brand of suicide, harakiri, in which the victim slits open his own stomach, is widespread.'

The picture of Japan which is prevalent today is no longer—or no longer exclusively—one of a strange and isolated country. Japan has passed through the Meiji reform period, has experienced the rapid rise and equally rapid collapse of a colonial power, has become actively involved in the sphere of world economy, and the increasing swarms of tourists who wing their way across the oceans have made the Land of the Rising Sun an integral part of our everyday world. But while the Japanese have impressed us with their readiness to accept all that is new in other parts of the world and to keep pace with the most advanced industrial nations, the foreigner is nevertheless left with the image of a country which has shown a unique capacity for clinging to the traditions which it built up over two thousand years. No nation has succeeded, as the Japanese have done, in preserving its national identity throughout its entire history. Japan never changed the dynasty which has ruled over it since mythical times, and not until the atomic age did it experience the presence of a foreign power on imperial soil.

The Land of the Gods

As early as the turn of the sixth century AD, when the country known to historians emerged, Japan seems already to have acquired a high degree of national unity. Its more remote origins, by contrast, are obscure. Popular tradition, which at least has the virtue of simplicity, has it that all that remained of the original inhabitants—the Ainu who lived in a few villages in the northern island Hokkaido—were driven out by the main Mongol branch of the Japanese, who moved in comparatively late. We know today, however, that there was a whole series of immigrations which continued, in fact, until the early centuries of the Christian era, and presumably the Tenno clan, which eventually dominated Yamato (site of the modern Nara), came in on one of the last waves. Earlier immigrations, however, covered a period of thousands of years, and even the Ainu, who were once represented in large numbers on the main island Honshu, are not the original inhabitants of Japan.

Skull-measurements, language research and comparisons of Japan's rich mythology with that of other peoples have suggested a whole variety of lines of racial affinity, extending to Melanesia and by way of Formosa to the Malay Archipelago, but principally through the Korean peninsula both to southern China and northwards to Siberia and farther west. One theory, which is still being mooted, even suggests that there are striking similarities in their respective ancient traditions which point to the Japanese and the Jewish people in Mesopotamia having a common origin.

In 1949 at Kanto in the Gunma prefecture primitive stone implements were excavated, which extended the frontiers of Japan's known prehistory by several thousands of years back to the Palæolithic Age. More discoveries of this kind were made, but so far no human remains by which to identify the race to which these early inhabitants belonged. It can be assumed that in the area known today as Japan men were living in the primeval forests at a time when there was still a land bridge connecting it with the Asian continent.

We know more about the Jomon culture, named after the cord-impressed pottery of a people of food-gatherers and hunters in the Neolithic period, who have also been traced to the northern and southern mainland as well as to Melanesia. The development of this culture from the vessels with pointed bases of the first period to the clay figures of the fifth period extended over thousands of years.

Around 300 BC the Yayoi culture emerged, the first examples of which were discovered in the Yayoi-cho quarter of Tokyo. Presumably it is related to a fresh wave of immigrants, who brought with them the first specimens of Chinese culture, which was already highly developed. From then on a more advanced process was employed for firing pottery, metal implements appeared for the first time, fishing and shipping were developed and, above all, the introduction of rice-cultivation gave rise to sedentary peasant communities.

The first centuries of the Christian era are shrouded in a sort of historical twilight. Japanese folklore with its fantastic conception of time—many of Japan's early rulers are alleged to have reigned for over a century—contrasts sharply with the occasional early references to Japan in the much more reliable Chinese annals. In the *Kansho*, the book of the Han dynasty which dates back to around AD 92, Japan is referred to as 'Wa'. Towards the end of the second century BC Wa is reputed to have had more than a hundred *kuni* or tribes and to have sent envoys to China every year. The book of the later Han dynasty, *Go-Kansho*, mentions a visit by envoys from the Nu-no-Kuni tribe to the court of Loyang. In the *Gishi*, the chronicle of the Wei dynasty, there are reports of *kuni* fighting in Yamato at the end of the second century.

The emergence of the warlike people amongst whom the Tenno clan achieved a dominating position is not recorded until the third or fourth centuries. The first outstanding figure to appear was the legendary Empress Jingo, who possessed powerful shamanistic attributes. Following the sudden death of her husband, she embarked, in an advanced state of pregnancy, on an invasion of Korea and on her return gave birth to the next emperor Ojin. In the fifth century the Tennos had become so firmly established in Yamato, that the Japanese ruler was able to claim in a letter to the Chinese imperial court in 478, which is quoted in the *Sojo*, book of the Sung dynasty: 'Our forefathers, well armed, undertook military expeditions into the wilderness and subdued 55 states in east Japan including Ezo and 66 states in the west, among them Kumaso. Further they crossed the sea and subjected 95 states in Korea.'

In the fifth and sixth centuries the superior Chinese culture began to exercise an increasingly powerful influence in the island. Around the year 400, Koreans introduced the Chinese script, in the middle of the sixth century Chinese classics and medical books became known, the pervasive influence of Confucianism started to make itself felt in government circles, the message of Buddha, the Enlightened, was spread abroad, and finally, influenced by the Chinese sense of history, the Japanese made their first attempts to record their own past. Two of these accounts have survived: the *Kojiki*, presented to the Tenno by its author O-no-Yasumaro in 712, and the *Nihonshoki*, which was completed in 720. Both begin with the story of the Creation, which was so important as an explanation of the origins of the Japanese imperial family and which reveals the profound significance of mythology to the Japanese. We propose therefore to look at the origins of the 'Land of the Gods' and its 'Son of Heaven' as presented in the *Kojiki* a little more closely, rather than contenting themselves with the usual cursory statement that the Tenno originated with the sun goddess Amaterasu—a theory which until 1945 was the official State doctrine.

X *In the Higashi-Honganji Temple of Kyoto, centre of the younger branch of the Shin sect, a commemoration festival, lasting several days, with processions and ritual dances is held every fifty years in memory of the patriarch Shinran Sho-nin, who died in 1262 (see also colour plate XXIII and ill. 163)*

The Story of the Creation

When chaos had begun to gather but neither original force nor form, nothing concrete or created had yet appeared, who could have recognized the shape of the universe? Then heaven and earth began to separate from one another and in the realms of the High Heavens the Lord of the lofty centre of the heavens *Ame no Minaka-nushi* and the two other, equally invisible divinities *Takami-musubi* and *Kami-musubi* emerged. When thereafter the land was young and jelly-fish drifted on the primeval ocean like floating oil, there arose from a thing that sprouted forth like the young shoot of a reed two more invisible gods. These are the Five Special Gods of Heaven.

Now the two invisible divinities emerged, 'The One Standing on the Earth' and the 'Abundantly Germinating Lord'. They were followed by several divine couples of brothers and sisters, the fifth being *Izanagi* (Inviting Lord) and *Izanami* (Inviting Woman). These are the Seven Generations of the Age of the Gods.

The Gods of Heaven hand Izanagi and Izanami a spear studded with jewels and command them: 'Create, establish and make complete the land drifting about there below!' The couple thrust the spear down from the Suspended Bridge of Heaven and stir the salt waters until they grow thick. When Izanagi and Izanami withdraw the spear, the salt water dripping from its point forms the island of *Onogoro* (the self-congealing). The two gods descend to this island, thrust the heavenly spear into the ground and use it as the central pillar of a hall, which they build round it.

Izanagi asks his younger sister: 'How is thy body formed?' She replies: 'My body grows and grows continually, only there is one part which does not grow continually.' Thereupon Izanagi: 'My body grows and grows continually, but there is one part which grows to excess. It is therefore good if I insert this part of my body which is growing to excess in that part of your body which is not growing and, thus procreating, bring forth countries.'

They move round the heavenly pillar in opposite directions, and Izanami greets her brother with the words: 'O beautiful, lovely youth!' But he replies: 'It is not proper that the woman should speak first.'

The first child they produce is accordingly misconceived: it is a son, *Hiru-ko* (leech). They place him in a reed-boat and let it drift away. The second birth, the island of Aha (island of shame), also gives them no joy. The couple turn to the gods for advice. With instructions to mend their speech, they return to the hall and once again walk round the heavenly pillar. But now it is Izanagi who greets his sister first: 'Ah! how beautiful! What a lovely maiden!' The next child is the island *Ahaji no Ho-no-sa-wake* and the ensuing one the island *Ivo-no-Futama* with four faces on one body. In this way a whole series of islands is created, among them the 'richly autumnal island Great Yamato'.

After the islands, the divine couple produce ten deities, among them the god of the sea and the god of estuaries together with his younger sister, who bears him eight more water-gods. Thus are born the wind-god, the tree-god, the mountain-god, the field-god, and from the union of mountain- and field-god come a further eight deities. Finally Izanagi and Izanami produce three more children but, in giving birth to the third, the fire-god, Izanami's pudenda are burnt and she falls mortally sick. From the matter eliminated from her body emerge the two deities of the iron mountain.

XI The manufacture of the sword as the noblest of weapons was developed to a fine art, particularly from the 14th century onwards, and even the most exalted person, including the Emperor, practised forging the steel-blade.

Izanagi speaks: 'Oh! Thou my lovely younger sister Highness! Oh! That I should have exchanged thee for one single child!' He creeps round her pillow and round her feet and from his tears is created the 'The Weeping One', a deity who lives in the mountains. After Izanami's death Izanagi draws his sword and cuts off the head of his son, the fire-god. From the blood that clings to the sword eight deities are born and eight more emerge from the limbs of the victim.

Izanagi searches in the underworld for his departed wife. When she appears before him at the entrance to the underworld, he calls to her: 'Thou my beloved younger sister Highness! The lands which I and thou have created are not yet completed. Therefore return!' Izanami replies: 'Alas! Thou shouldst have come earlier! For I have eaten of the food of the underworld.' She promises none the less to enquire of the deities of the underworld whether it is not still possible for her to return. A condition is that he must on no account look for her.

Izanami returns to the palace of the underworld and Izanagi waits. When he grows tired of waiting, he breaks a tooth from his comb, lights it and goes with it through the gate to seek Izanami. There he sees her body, decayed and eaten by worms, from which eight gods of thunder have been formed. He starts back horrified, but Izanami calls to him: 'Thou hast shamed me!' She looses the Hideous Women of the Underworld on him. Izanagi throws his black head-cloth towards them, which immediately changes into bunches of grapes, and the women devour these while he flees. But soon they are after him again. Now he takes the many-toothed comb from his hair and, as he throws it down, bamboo-shoots spring from it, which again distract the women. Izanami then sends the eight gods of thunder together with five hundred warriors from the underworld in pursuit of her brother. He defends himself by swinging his great sword behind him and so reaches the slope on the borders of the underworld. There he plucks three fruits from a peach-tree and throws them at his pursuers, who thereupon all take flight. But now Izanami approaches, menacing. Izanagi bars her way with a rock and calls out the formal phrase signifying divorce. Izanami replies: 'Thou my beloved husband and Highness! If thou doest such a thing, I shall kill in one day a thousand heads from the human grass of thy country!' To which Izanagi replies: 'Thou my beloved younger sister and Highness! If thou doest such a thing, I shall build one thousand five hundred birth-huts in one day. Then a thousand people will die and a thousand five hundred will be born in one day.'

In order to cleanse himself from contact with the impure world of death, Izanagi now repairs to the River Woto in Tsukushi (Kyushu). From the garments and effects which he discards for bathing twelve new deities are formed, and a further fourteen deities emerge from the purification itself. From the washing of the left eye comes *Amaterasu-Omikami*, from the washing of the right eye *Tsukiyomi*, and from the washing of the nose *Takehaya-Susanowo*. Overjoyed at the birth of these last three children, Izanagi hands Amaterasu his jewel-studded collar with the words: 'Your Highness shall rule over the domains of High Heaven!' To Tsukiyami he says: 'Your Highness shall be master over the land that dominates the Night!' And to Susanowo: 'Your Highness shall rule over the domains of the ocean!'

Susanowo is not satisfied with this decision. He seeks out his sister, ostensibly to take leave of her, and makes this proposal: 'Let us both take an oath and produce children.' Thereupon Amaterasu takes her brother's great sword, breaks it into three parts, washes them in the spring of heaven by brandishing them to and fro, while the jewels that bedeck them make a jingling sound, then chews them with a crunching sound and spits them out. The mist of her breath congeals into three female deities. Susanowo for his part accepts the jewels worn by Amaterasu, chews them with a crunching sound and blows them away, whereupon five male deities appear. Amaterasu decrees that the children produced from her jewels belong to her, while those created from the sword belong to her brother. The three new female deities take up their abode in island sanctuaries, but the five males become the ancestors of earthly races.

Susanowo's misdeeds become so excessive that Amaterasu shuts herself up in the darkness of her palace and thus denies the world the light of the sun. The other deities, who amuse themselves with all manner of mischief, succeed in enticing her out again by means of the sacred mirror, which has since been fashioned, and the sacred jewelled necklace. Susanowo, however, is condemned by the eight hundred myriads of supernatural spirits and is deprived of his beard. He asks the Goddess of Nourishment *Oho-ge-tsu-hime* for food. She takes from the various parts of her body all kinds of tasty morsels, but Susanowo considers them unclean and kills the goddess. From her head emerges the silkworm, in the two eyes appear the first grains of rice, in the ears millet, in the nose the adzuki bean (*Phassolus radiatus*), inher puden-da barley and in her posterior the soya bean.

Susanowo descends to the earth and in the land of Izume encounters an earthly couple whose daughter is in danger of being devoured by a giant snake with eight heads. He changes the daughter into a comb and makes the giant snake drunk with rice-wine, then kills it with his sword. In its body he finds the sacred sword, *Kusanagino-tsurugi* the 'grass-mowing sword' which Prince Yamato uses to subdue his enemies.

Thereafter Susanowo lives in his palace at Suga in Izume and involves the deities living on the earth in a bewildering succession of fantastic events, until finally Amaterasu in conjunction with *Takami-musubi* (one of the three invisible gods, with whom the creation of the world began—he now appears invariably at the side of the sun-goddess) sends down her son and heir to take over control of the earth: this is *Masaka-a-Katsu Katchi-Hayabi Abe no Oshi-ho-mimi no Mikoto* ('the all-conquering great exalted Person of Heaven of the truly victorious triumphant fierce demeanour'), the first of the five gods who emerged from Amaterasu's jewels after they had been chewed and spat out by Susanowo. While the heir to the throne is preparing to come down to earth, a son is born to him: *Ame-nigishi kuni-nigishi Ama-tsu-hi-daka Hiko-ho no Ninigi* ('heavenly-abundant earthly-abundant heaven-sun-high exalted prince—scion-red-abundant'), in abbreviated form *Hiko-ho no Ninigi no Mikoto*. To him is given the command: 'Descend to this land of fresh shoots and the luxuriant reed-fields, for this is the land over which you shall rule.' Amaterasu gives him her Yasaka jewels, the sacred mirror and the grass-mowing sword, and as companions she gives him the five chiefs (of the various tribes).

Hiko-ho no Ninigi no Mikoto encounters the pretty daughter of a mountain-god. To his question: 'I would like to wed thee, what dost thou think?' she gives the appropriate reply: 'My humble self cannot say. My humble self's father will tell thee.' The mountain-god is delighted and promptly gives the elder sister as well. But, as she is ugly, Hiko-ho sends her back. The father, furious, explains to him why he would have done well to take both daughters: 'In sending you my elder daughter, I wished her to ensure for ever and all time the life of the exalted descendants, however often the snow might fall and the wind blow, but the younger daughter would give the exalted descendants a rich life like the blossoming of trees. As you have now sent back the elder daughter and kept only the younger, the life of the exalted descendants will be as fleeting as tree-blossoms.'

From this union with the daughter of the mountain-god sprang *Hoderi no Mikoto* (the ancestor of the Haya-hito of Satsuma), *Hosuseri no Mikoto* and *Howori no Mikoto*. Howori weds the daughter of the sea-god and spends three years in his palace. He subdues his eldest brother Hoderi. During her confinement in a hut hastily built of reeds, the daughter of the sea-god turns into a sea-monster and gives birth to *Amatsu-Hidaka-hiko Nagisa-take U-gaya-fuki-ahezu no Mikoto* ('high prince of the son of heaven, valiant cormorant (feather) of the sea-shore-unfinished one of the reed-roof'). Howori lives for the next 580 years in the palace of Takachiho in the land of Himuka (Kyushu). His son *U-gaya-firki-ahezu* marries his mother's younger sister and from this union come *Itsutso, Inahi, Mikenu* and finally *Waka-Mineku*, who is also called *Toyo-Mineku* or *Kamu-Yamato Ihare-Biko*. The third son Mikenu steps onto the crest of a wave and enters the land of immortality. The second son Inahi goes to the region of the seas, the country of his deceased mother. The eldest and the youngest brothers, Itsuso and Yamato Ihare live, to begin with, in their father's palace at Takachiho, then at Usa in the land of Tojo, then at Takeri in the land of Agie, then at Takashima in the land of Kibi. Itsuse dies at Kawachi, struck by the arrow of a native prince, and of the four brothers only Yamato Ihare remains, who is none other than the legendary first emperor, *Jimmu*.

In the village of Kumano, Yamato Ihare together with his warriors becomes unconscious. Takakuraji from Kumano brings him a broad sword and he awakes again. A crow sent by the god Takagi accompanies Yamato Ihare further and after a series of adventures he reaches Uda and Osaka. By the mountain called Unebi at Yamato he moves into the Kashibara Palace. At Himuka he has married Ahira-hime, who bears him *Tagishi-mimi*. He reaches an age of 137 years. His successor Tagishi marries Isuke-yorihime, who later becomes his father's wife, but he attempts to take the life of her three sons, his step-brothers: the two younger ones try to forestall him. The elder of the two, selected for the task, trembles so much that he cannot deliver the fatal blow, and he enters the priesthood, after the youngest has done the deed for him. But the fratricide becomes ruler of the earth.

Shotoku Taishi's Seventeen Articles

In the year AD 593—we are now on fairly solid historical ground—the Empress Suiko ascended the throne as the thirty-third Tenno, but she left the responsibility of government to her nephew *Umayado-no-toyotomimi-no-mikoto*, who has become known by his posthumous name Shotoku Taishi. During his twenty-eight years as Prince Regent, against the background of the old family and tribal units, the outlines of the empire began to emerge with its custom-based claim to universality. Under Shotoku Taishi Japan, following the great example set by China, became a civilized nation almost overnight, and, as has happened with other men of his stature, legend contributed considerably to his image. There is hardly a single achievement during this period that has not been ascribed to his religious, statesmanlike and artistic genius. Shotoku encouraged the Chinese influence and himself became immersed in the Buddhist doctrine; but he was too Japanese to surrender anything of the tradition of his ancestors and, while a Buddhist temple was built at Horyuji, the worship at the Shinto shrines of Ise built by the Empress Sujin was not neglected. Shotoku compared Shinto to the root, Confucianism to the trunk and Buddhism to the fruit of one and the same tree.

Around the year 604 Shotoku Taishi embodied his doctrine of the State and society in the seventeen articles of the *Jushichijo-kempo*. After the indigenous story of the creation in the *Kami* with its countless gods, which still pursue their ghostly lives in nature to this day, came the orderly spirit of man, as Confucius had proclaimed it a thousand years before in the middle kingdom as the heir to the wise rulers of ancient times. Henceforth the patriarchal system in Japan was always based on Shotoku's Seventeen Articles and it continued to draw enough strength from them to survive almost to this day. So it seems appropriate to reproduce them here in full as representing, in sharp contrast to the myth of creation recounted a century later in the *Kojiki* and the *Nihonshoki*, the other basic ingredient of any picture of Japan.

FIRST ARTICLE

Harmony *(wa)* is the highest.

Non-rebelliousness of those below against those above and of those above against those below: this is what matters.

Men cling to their own desires and only a few are capable of serving the cause alone.

So it comes about that they do not obey the Prince's or the Father's wishes and that they come into conflict with their neighbours.

But when there is harmony *(wa)* above and open-heartedness *(boku)* below and when in both places the same words are employed, then reason, which is inherent in things, prevails.

What can then possibly fail?

SECOND ARTICLE

Honour with your whole heart the three jewels!

The three jewels are the Buddha, the teaching *(dharma)*, and the order.

They are the final refuge of the four kinds of Being and the meaning of the Ten Thousand Kingdoms.

Which age, which men should not hold this teaching sacred?

Few men are by nature bad.

By instruction those who err can be led back to the path of the teaching.

But how can one make the crooked straight without having recourse to the three jewels?

THIRD ARTICLE

Having received the word of the Emperor, reflect upon it reverently.

The Prince *(kun)* is like to the heavens, the led *(shin)* like to the earth.

The heavens cover, the earth bears:

So the Four Seasons go their ordered way

And the Ten Thousand Affairs are resolved.

But if the earth tries to raise itself above the heavens, the world will fall apart.

The Prince speaks, the led receives.

Above is the cause, below the effect.

Therefore: After receiving the word of the Emperor, consider it well.

Lack of respectful attention leads to destruction.

FOURTH ARTICLE

The Princes and the Hundred Offices have morals *(li)* for their basic principle.

It is on morals that the guidance of the people depends.

If morals are not observed by those above, then corruption will spread.

If therefore the Prince and the servants of the State follow morals, rank and order are preserved.

If the people has morals, the Empire governs itself.

FIFTH ARTICLE

Renounce greed, throw your passions away.

Let your judgement in quarrels be incorruptible and clear.

A thousand quarrels break out among the people in one single day,

How many more there must be as the years mount up!

Now it comes to pass, as has indeed always been the case, that those who govern look to their own profit,

They look for gifts, before they pass judgement.

And so, when someone with money is on trial, it is as if a stone were thrown into the water,

And when someone without money is on trial, it is as if water were thrown on a stone:

Then the poor people does not know where to turn and order is undermined.

SIXTH ARTICLE

To suppress evil and promote good is the wise rule of the old.

Therefore do not let the good remain hidden, and, where you see evil, set it right.

Those who speak falsely, whether they flatter or whether they deceive, are a dangerous instrument, with which they undermine the Empire—they are a sharp sword, with which they bring ruin to the people.

Flatterers know how to acquaint those above with the mistakes of those below,

And they gossip to those below of the mistakes of those above:

Such men are lacking in loyalty to the Princes and to their own kind,

They are the roots of general disorder.

SEVENTH ARTICLE

Each man has his own vocation.

Introduce no confusion into this!

Do wise men hold office, then terhe is endless praise.

But do unworthy men hold office, then misfortune and chaos spread.

While only few are born wise, it is open to many through earnest endeavour to become wise.

Everything, whether great or small, finds its place, if the just man looks after his own.

At all times, be they peaceful or out of joint, everything resolves itself if a wise man is at the helm:

Then the Empire has continuity and the country is free from danger.

That is why the sacred kings of old sought the man for the office, not the office for the man.

EIGHTH ARTICLE

The Great and the Hundred Offices shall go early to the Court and leave late.

The affairs of the Empire brook no delay,

A long day is barely sufficient to conduct them.

If one comes too late to the Court, it may be too late for urgent affairs.

If one leaves too early, important matters remain unresolved.

NINTH ARTICLE

Loyalty (*hsin*—belief, trust) is the root of justice.

Loyalty shall always prevail.

Success or failure in anything depends on loyalty.

If those above and those who are led remain loyal to one other, everything will resolve itself,

But if those above and those who are led are lacking in loyalty, the Ten Thousand Affairs will miscarry.

TENTH ARTICLE

Have done with your ill humour, cast aside your anger,

Do not hold it against others if they think otherwise.

Each man follows his own 'I' with his own inclinations.

If the other is right, then I am wrong, and if I am right, then the other is wrong.

I am not simply the wise man and the other the fool—we are both men.

Who can decide where justice lies and where injustice?

Wisdom and foolishness are intertwined as in an endless circle.

So when someone is angry with us, let us consider where our own shortcomings lie.

If, however, we feel we are in the right, this is no reason for us to behave differently from the others.

ELEVENTH ARTICLE

Examine well where merit lies and where guilt, and make it known!

Distribute reward and punishment without ulterior motive!

All too often reward does not result from merit or punishment from guilt. Therefore those responsible should pay more heed to the just attribution of reward and punishment!

TWELFTH ARTICLE

The *kuni* (dignitaries operating in specific regions) should not levy duties or taxes for themselves.

In the Empire there cannot be two kinds of ruler, and the people should not have two kinds of master.

Every inch of land and every inhabitant have only one Emperor, and the dignitaries are all delegates of the one Emperor.

How could they therefore dare to levy tributes for themselves as if they were the rulers?

THIRTEENTH ARTICLE

All who are entrusted with an office should fulfil their duties in the same way.

If they are prevented by illness or extraneous affairs from performing their office, they should resume their customary duties as quickly as possible.

XII *In a niche of the Yomei-mon, the magnificent gate leading to the Toshogu Shrine at Nikko (ills. 105–107), the second of Japan's three Great Unifiers, Toyotomi Hideyoshi (1530–1598), is represented as a knightly archer.*

Do not impede the progress of public affairs on the pretext of your ignorance!

FOURTEENTH ARTICLE

You in the Hundred Offices, banish envy and jealousy!

If I persecute others with my envy, they will persecute me with theirs.

There is no telling what mischief may spring from envy and jealousy.

If the other is superior in insight, discontent results; if he is superior in talent, envy and jealousy result.

In five hundred years you may meet one wise man, in a thousand years hardly a single saint.

But without the wise man, without the saint—how can one govern the Empire?

FIFTEENTH ARTICLE

Let the servant of the State overcome his selfishness and keep the common good alone in mind.

Where selfishness prevails, ill-will results.

Where ill-will prevails, discord results.

Where discord prevails, selfishness impedes public affairs.

Ill-will leads to violation of the regulations and laws.

If therefore in the First Article harmony from above and below is demanded, that also applies here.

SIXTEENTH ARTICLE

To implicate the people (in duties) only at the appropriate time was a sound principle of the ancients.

Therefore: In the winter months the people have leisure and can then be implicated.

From spring until autumn, however, is the time for cultivating the fields and for tending the mulberry-trees, so the people cannot be implicated.

For, if the fields are not cultivated, what shall we eat? And if the mulberry trees are not tended (for the cultivation of silk), what shall we wear?

XIII–XIV *The Nijo Palace at Kyoto was built by Tokugawa Ieyasu, founder of the Edo shogunate, as the residence of the shogun and his representative in the old capital. The grounds, surrounded by walls and a moat and covering an area of 70 acres, gives one some idea of the splendour of a prince's palace in the early 17th century. The entrance to the reception rooms is decorated with coloured wood-carvings of peonies and phoenixes ascribed to the sculptor Hidari Jingoro. In 1868 the palace was the provisional seat of the new government and it was from here that the Emperor Meiji proclaimed the abolition of the shogunate. The emblem of the Tokugawa shoguns—aoi leaves—on the roof-ridges was replaced by the imperial chrysanthemum.*

Great decisions should not be the concern of one man alone.

They require consultation with others.

In small things it is easier, there discussion by many is not necessary.

But when big things are at stake, the danger of error is great—therefore many should discuss and clarify the matter together, so that the correct way may be found!

Emperors and Regents

The political and military history of Japan is not merely unique in that the ruling dynasty, once it was established, never changed. No less unusual is the fact that for twelve centuries hardly any mention is made of relations with other nations. Apart from occasional attacks on the Korean mainland, there were no foreign wars until the latter part of the 19th century. Hideyoshi's dramatic attempt to conquer China collapsed in face of the concentrated power of the Ming armies and after the death of the powerful general no further attempt was made until the military clique took over in the 20th century. On the other hand, in historical times only one attempt was made to invade Japan, by the Mongols after their conquest of China. But their fleet was scattered by a storm and the first landing by a foreign army was only made in 1945 after the atom bomb had forced the Japanese to capitulate.

From time to time Japan developed extremely fruitful religious and cultural relations with China, but on the political and diplomatic level the only contact was the occasional despatch of a Japanese mission to the Chinese imperial court. The ruler of the Middle Kingdom, for whom the very existence of foreign sovereign States was inconceivable, looked upon the gifts brought to him as the tribute of some remote vassal, and at a time when the Tenno was concerned to improve his status in the island-empire, he was quite happy to accept from the distant ruler of the world an honorary title such as Ch'iang-chün, which later became the Japanese Shogun, but the Chinese never tried to assert their sovereignty in any other way.

Although the stage seemed to be set for a remarkably homogeneous development, the history of Japan is not without its periods of violent upheaval. In centuries of continuous civil war bloody battles were fought between the most powerful of the generals each with his tribal supporters, and, despite the inviolability of their imperial overlord, the actual exercise of supreme power in the Empire was bitterly contested and led to every conceivable form of regency.

The designation of the Tenno as 'Son of Heaven' is a reminder of the influence of China in the evolution of the Japanese imperial system. In China, as in India, the idea of laying claim to an empire which embodied the entire known world also carried with it the even wider concept of an earthly institution which represented the divine world-order. The Japanese developed this idea in their own special way.

The Chinese Emperor was the absolute head of a huge state-pyramid, which was based on moral principles. As Son of Heaven he wielded unlimited power, but Heaven could always deny him its favours. If the ruler was no longer able to maintain order in his dominions, then he had forfeited his divine mission and his functions were taken over by the man whom Providence had chosen to seize firmly the reins of government and form a new dynasty. But the Japanese Tenno was the descendant and heir of a deity and the mandate of the ruling house was as inalienable as its divine descent. On the other hand, the Tenno's power was never absolute. He derived his position from being the supreme head of the most powerful tribe in the ancient Yamato, whose role as priests and arbiters was recognized by an ever-increasing circle of the *uji* or clans. But there were also other powerful tribes which could claim partial descent from the gods, although not on such an exalted level as the Tenno, and new, influential clans even emerged from branches of the imperial family itself. The Taika Edict of 646, and the reforms that followed, tried to set up a centralized imperial system on the Chinese model but tribal regionalism kept reasserting itself and until recent times continued to be one of the decisive factors in Japanese history.

It is symptomatic that the very first outstanding personalities in Japanese history, the legendary Empress Jingo and the Prince Regent Shotoku Taishi, did not assume the title of Tenno. Nevertheless under the early emperors there were several rulers, such as Temmu (672–687) and Kammu (781–806), the founder of Kyoto, who left their own individual mark on the age in which they lived. The Tenno was more and more committed to an exhausting round of ceremonial and confined to the environment of the court. It became accepted practice for the ruler to assume his high office while he was still a child and to abdicate more or less voluntarily when he had barely reached manhood. So it was not uncommon to find one or more exemperors living in Kyoto at the same time as the ruling Tenno and, in some cases, exercising a greater influence than when they occupied the throne. The ex-emperor received the honorary title *joko* (Elder Emperor) or, if he entered the priesthood, *hoo* (Buddhist: King of the Law). To an ambitious Tenno abdication was the long-awaited opportunity to gain real, personal power. For example under Go-Sanjo, following his abdication in 1073, the *in-no-cho* or 'Office of the Abdicated Emperor' was set up, which remained for the next seventy years the centre of political power. Go-Daigo, who ascended the throne in 1318, tried to revert to the system under which the emperor assumed control of state affairs, but immediately became involved in the violent conflict between the generals and for fifty-six years Japan was divided into northern and southern imperial courts.

The office in which the supreme powers of the Empire were invested did not always bear the same name; very often it depended on personalities and circumstances whether one or another of the imperial offices took the operative decisions.

The history of the actual rulers is one of clans as much as of personalities. Under Shotoku Taishi, for example, the *Soga*, who played an important part in the establishment of Buddhism as the State religion, were at the height of their power, but under Shotoku's successor they were ousted. *Nakatomi-no-Kamatari* (614–669), who was partly responsible for the Taika Reforms and who received from the Tenno the honorary family name of Fujiwara, ushered in two centuries of domination by his lineage. The *mandokoro*, an administrative body run by the Fujiwara, became the real seat of government during the Heian period. (See the chronological table at the end of the book.) Fujiwara Fuyutsugu, as *kur-odo-no-kami*, was 'Head of the Emperor's Privy Council', and in 857 his son Yoshifusa was appointed *dajo-daijin* or 'Head of the Council for Worldly Affairs', besides which there was another council responsible for ritual affairs. The family had improved their position still further by marrying into the imperial house and in 858, when

Yoshifusa's own grandson Seiwa ascended the throne, he adopted the title of *sessho*, which was also borne by subsequent regents where the Emperor was a minor. His successor as head of the Fujiwara family, Mototsuna, even went a step further when, after he had been regent to two emperors under age, he created in 884, the post of *kampaku*, who represented the Tenno, even after he had reached his majority, in dealing with officials. A kampaku who resigned could still be an influential man and was appointed *taiko*, a title made famous by Hideyoshi.

After the downfall of the Fujiwara there followed a period in which the wealthy monasteries became involved in the struggles for power and the imperial house, divided within itself, went into a decline, but before long the great clans with their vast estates reasserted their claim to control the affairs of the Empire. In the struggle between the Taira and the Minamoto victory went initially to the Taira. Kiyomori Taira, as Chancellor, bore the title of *juichii* from 1167 and, although he entered a monastic order the following year, he continued to hold the reins of government. But after his death the Minamoto renewed their challenge. The head of the family, Yoritomo, thanks to the military achievements of his kinsmen Yoshinaka and Yoshitsune, had built up a position of enormous power in Kamakura, from which he dominated the vast Kanto plain. He had himself appointed *so-shugo* and *sojito*, and finally in 1192 *shogun* or Generalissimo, by the Tenno, all titles which underlined the military character of his regime. The administrative centre was transferred to the *bakufu* (Field Headquarters) in Kamakura, far from the imperial capital Kyoto, where the courtiers spent their time cultivating the fine arts.

Three Minamoto shoguns ruled until 1219, when an ex-emperor Go-toba in Kyoto tried to regain power, but the bakufu in Kamakura, where a new clan had taken over, proved too strong for him.

From 1204 until 1333 the Hojo ruled, bearing the title of *skiken* and content to act as regents for the shogun. From 1226 onwards a shogun was once more appointed but he played much the same role as the Tenno in Kyoto. Frequently it was imperial princes, some still minors, who were called upon to fill the office and there were also abdicated or dethroned shoguns called *ogosho*.

Under the Tenno Go-daigo, while the imperial house was divided, the Ashikaga clan provided the shoguns and set up their headquarters in Muromachi, a quarter of Kyoto. With the establishment of imperial administrative bodies both in Kyoto and in Kamakura, each with a *kanryo* at its head, the area of conflict widened. The struggle for the shogunate and the rivalry between the autonomous territorial princes finally led to the civil war of the Sengoku period (1478–1577). Only when one powerful war-lord emerged in a dominant position did the central government regain its authority.

The first of the 'three great unifiers', Oda Nobunaga, was murdered by one of his own henchmen in 1582. He was followed by the most successful of his generals, Hideyoshi, on whom the Tenno bestowed the family name Toyotomi and the highest offices. After his death in 1598 his main rival, Tokugawa Ieyasu, founded the last great shogun dynasty, under which Japan was to enjoy Taihei, the Great Peace for the next two and a half centuries.

The reader who consults the chronological table will have to become familiar with yet another term, *nengo*, on which the dates of Japanese history are based. Nengo signifies a period of rule, which from the Meiji period onwards coincides with the reign of an emperor but which can also cover an arbitrary number of years, sometimes even only one, according to the prescription of the learned court soothsayers. Thus the Meiji era covers the forty-six-year reign of the Tenno who was posthumously named after his nengo, whereas the twenty-year reign of his predecessor Komei covers no less than six nengos of six, six, one, three, one and three years.

Religions and Sects

The terms which we have coined to cover our own realm of experience are frequently inadequate to describe the phenomena of other civilizations. What we usually call religions in East Asia do not always fit in with our own concept of religion, and when one speaks of sects in Japan, one must visualize not sectarian deviations from the great religious bodies but powerful and sometimes centuries-old doctrines and movements, which are more akin to our religious denominations or Churches. Statistical data also do not have the same significance as in the West where the population is divided into adherents of different religious faiths. Preference for a particular religious belief does not prevent the Japanese from revering other sects or even other religions, although he is not quite so starkly realistic as the pre-Maoist Chinese who, by donating joss-sticks in temples of every sect, hoped to insure himself against the risk of punishment in the Hereafter for having made a wrong choice. Only Christianity came into this world with the resolute claim to be exclusive.

Shinto, the 'Way of the Gods', is regarded as Japan's original religion. This is the doctrine of the *Kami*, the myriads of deities and spirits which people the universe and which are spoken of in the myth of the Creation. The Kami inhabit heaven, earth and the underworld, mountains, trees and water. They may be powerful gods or natural spirits of merely local importance, gods protecting specific places or clans, mighty armies of demons or the dead living on in the world of spirit.

Other peoples have shaken off nature-worship of this kind as they achieved a higher level of culture or have at least concealed it under the guise of a more sophisticated religion, but the Japanese are firmly wedded to their traditions and they also remained faithful to the 'Way of the Gods' even when they came in contact with the sublime wisdom of Indian and Chinese teachers and with the ruthless materialism of the West. The barbaric sacrifices of primitive times have of course long since been transformed into a sober and dignified ritual. Throughout the length and breadth of the country, from the hectic turmoil of the cities to the solitude of the mountains and forests, one finds the *torii*, the simple gateways, usually painted red, which stand at the entrance to a Shinto shrine. The gods love the stillness between the tall, old trees, and the clapping of hands raised in prayer is the appeal of a solitary creature to the mute majesty of nature. Any form of impurity, bodily or spiritual, is anathema to the gods.

As State religion Shintoism assimilated the Chinese idea of the Son of Heaven and the Universal Ruler and became the guardian of State morality, which finds its purest manifestation in loyalty to the Tenno. Reformers such as Hirata Atsutane (1776–1843) took great pains to keep Shintoism untainted by the constant incursion of foreign influences and made *sonno* (reverence for the imperial family) the key-note of their teaching.

In the Meiji period a distinction was drawn between Shrine Shinto (Jinja), whose priests were associated with the imperial cult and had official status, and Sect Shinto, which was practised in many different forms in the provinces. The shrines (so called to distinguish them from the Buddhist temples and Christian churches) were classified throughout the country and came under the Ministry of the Interior.

The Tenno's proclamation of 1946, inspired by the American proconsul, in which the State doctrine of the Tenno's divine descent was abandoned by the imperial house, dealt Shinto teaching a severe blow. But countless Japanese still visit the shrines, of which there are about 110,000, most of them belonging to the *Jinja Honcho* organization, and the Amaterasu shrine in the forest sanctuary at Ise, where the imperial insignia are preserved, is still a national place of pilgrimage.

Of the spiritual movements which reached Japan from the mainland with the introduction of the Chinese script, only Confucianism has left no visible traces. The Confucius temple in Tokyo, dating to the Tokugawa period, was already deserted in the Meiji period, and since 1945 the teaching of the Chinese moralist has disappeared from Japanese schoolbooks.

Kung-tse, who lived in the sixth century BC and became known in Europe by his latinized name Confucius, did not set out to found a religion but he did try through his teaching, which he saw translated into action by the wise kings of antiquity, to influence statesmen and the common people alike. Other wise men carried on his work and for over two thousand years left their mark on the structure of Chinese society. And hardly less enduring was Kung's influence on the patriarchal system of Japan, where the ancestor-cult managed to combine with the deep-rooted tribal economy and the Kami faith.

Confucian writings came to Japan as early as the Chinese Han Dynasty together with the Chinese script, and each reform movement in Confucianism on the mainland also spread to the island empire. Both the Seventeen Articles of the Prince Regent Shotoku Taishi and the principles formulated a thousand years later by Ieyasu Tokugawa are imbued with the Confucian spirit, which finally became accepted State theory in the *Shushi-gaku*. In a way that is characteristically Japanese, Shintoism, Confucianism and Buddhism mingled in all manner of forms. Since the Kamakura period Kung's moral precepts had exercised a salutary influence on *Bushido*, the code of honour of the warriors, and Zen priests propounded the view that the five commandments of Kung-tse were identical with those of the Buddha. Even as late as the Second World War the Japanese government tried to turn Kung's ethical precepts to account.

The Japanese also proved receptive to Chinese Taoism, but such traces as it left are more difficult to detect. The Taoist idea of achieving awareness by doing nothing while at the same time observing nature found its most sublime expression in the Japanese lyric, which captures all the peace and tranquillity of the temple garden.

Concurrently with the earliest infiltration of Chinese culture the religion deriving from the Indian *Shakyamuni* also came to Japan. Immediately after he had passed into nirvana as Buddha, the Enlightened, around 480 BC, his followers had summoned councils to reach agreement on the true doctrine but even at that early stage various rival schools began to form. Of the two main movements, the Hinayana or Little Vehicle and the Mahayana or Great Vehicle, the Mahayana gained most ground in East Asia, where it became part of the life of the people. This message from India brought to the world of natural spirits, of ancestor-worship and of man's role in the universal scheme of things a new element of the irrational—a true religion, which moved men's souls and released new inner forces.

Isolated Indian scholar-priests came to China and Chinese pilgrims undertook arduous journeys to the places where the historical Buddha had lived and worked and where, since then, the traditional sutras had been studied in large monasteries. And before long the teachings, which had been so successful in China, spread through an exchange of priests to Japan.

From the many sects which were formed around individual priests and monasteries emerged the three main schools to which the majority of Japanese belong today: the sect of the Pure Land, which worships the Redeemer-Buddha Amida, the Zen sects which go back to the Chinese school of meditation Ch'an-tsung, and the Lotus sects founded by the monk Nichiren.

Amida or Amitabha (having immeasurable brilliance) was an Indian monk who became a Buddha. He governs the Pure Land (Sukhavati), the Paradise in the West; there he receives all believers, who through his instruction seek to find salvation.

The Pure Land school, in Chinese *Ching-t'u-tsung*, was introduced into China by the Indian scholar Sanghavarman, who translated the great Amitayus sutra. Later, other Amida sutras were translated and annotated, and, after the Japanese Tendai priest Ryonin had in the year 1117 made Amida the focal point of worship in his temple at Osaka, this school of the 'shorter road to salvation' gained in popularity in Japan.

The monk Honen, founder of the *Jodo-shu* sect which is still popular today, explains his teaching as follows:

'However many gates (directions or teachings) there are through which one treads the way of Buddha, renouncing this world of sorrows, all can be divided into two directions. These are *Sho-do-mon* and *Jo-do-mon*, the Gate of the Sacred Path and the Gate of the Pure Land.

'Sho-do-mon, the Gate of the Sacred Path is the way by which, even while one is living here below in this world, one casts out all sin and attains enlightenment. Here there are two branches, namely *Mahayana-Shodo* and *Hinayana-Shodo*, the Sacred Path of the Great Vehicle and the Sacred Path of the Little Vehicle. And both are again divided into two classes, which are together called the four Yana. But they are altogether unsuitable for such as ourselves in this present time... The Gate of the Sacred Path we can simply dismiss from our minds, remembering that this teaching is hard for us to grasp who are so far removed in time from the days of the founder, and that the way it points is beyond our powers and will all too early lead us into error.

'The so-called *Jo-do-mon*, the Gate of the Pure Land, on the other hand, directs us to abandon this world and to be born with all possible speed into the Blissful Realm. But a pre-condition for being born into this land is the sworn promise of the Buddha Amida, the choice among men being made regardless of whether they are good or bad. No, of this alone is account taken, whether a man believes in this promise of the Buddha...

'This Shodo and this Jodo we call the Way of Hard Practice and the Way of Easy Practice. To make it clear by the old comparison: the Way of Hard Practice is to be compared with a journey on foot along rough paths. The Way of Easy Practice, on the other hand, is like a journey across the sea on a ship. He who is lame in the legs or who is blind may not seek to reach the goal by the first way; he can only reach the shore on the other side, if he is transported on a ship. But we who live in these days are, after all, only human, our eyes blinded to wisdom, our legs lamed to the pursuit of the commandments. It is therefore not even thinkable for us that we might set our hopes on the Way of Hard Practice to which Shodo directs us. No, if we wish to cross the Samsara Ocean of life and death to the shore of the Blissful Realm, then we can only do this if we cross by ship, on Amida's solemn vow.'

The *Ch'an* or Zen teaching imposes much greater demands on the believer. It too attaches no particular value to the study of holy writ or to good deeds, and ritual is of secondary importance to the need for complete absorption in the eternal cosmos. The goal which the Zen acolyte sets himself is 'intuitive awareness of the Buddha-nature of one's own spirit, the experience of the identity of all existing things in the eternally peaceful All-One.' At the same time Taoism demands concentration on the essence of truth undisturbed by the world of appearances. Strict exercises in meditation help the monk to overcome selfish desires and protect him against distractions of any kind.

As a school of self-discipline, free from all impure and unnatural elements, the Zen teaching covers every sphere of activity, and in the Kamakura period it produced a new elite of warriors, poets, painters and gardeners. The Zen monasteries were among the most distinguished fostering-grounds of Japanese culture and they preserved their ideals throughout the restless years of the civil war and the long period of peace under the Tokugawa right up to the present time.

The third group of Japanese Buddhists is entirely dominated by the extraordinary personality of the founder, Yakuomaru, who was born in 1222, became the prophet of Japan, and called himself Nichiren, the 'Sun Lotus'. As a twelve-year-old boy he prayed that he might become the wisest man in Japan. The young monk immersed himself in the teachings of all the various sects and travelled from monastery to monastery until finally, at the age of thirty-one, he found salvation in the worship of the Lotus Sutra. He then proceeded to proclaim his teaching throughout the country with remarkable eloquence. He not only accused the existing religious communities of having failed, he also denounced corruption in the State and thereby aroused the hostility of those in power. He was frequently arrested and exiled and on one occasion only escaped execution by a near-miracle. His religious admonitions and promises were accompanied by a passionate appeal to the nation to undergo a complete regeneration—and the threat of a Mongol invasion lent an alarming topicality to his prophetic words.

Nichiren's standing is as high today as it ever was and a wave of militancy has swept through the millions of Japanese Buddhists who look upon him as one of the greatest of their national leaders.

The visitor to Japan's temples and monasteries, who is overwhelmed by the sheer variety of artistic and spiritual activity, will find himself confronted by many different manifestations of Buddhism. The following catalogue of the principal sects will, it is hoped, help to make the over-all picture a little clearer:

THE SIX SECTS OF THE NARA PERIOD (NANTO ROKUSHU)

Sanron: introduced by the Korean Ekwan in 625, based on the Chinese 'School of the three Texts' (*San-lun-tsung*), which goes back to the *Madhyamikashastra* of the south Indian Nagarjuna. Has died out in Japan. Main centre was Horyuji.

Hosso: introduced by the Japanese monk Dosho, pupil of Hsüan-tsang, made famous by his pilgrimage to India, and of the Dharma-lakshana school or Yuishiki, which he represented. The sect owns the monasteries of Horyuji, Kokofuji and Yakushiji (Nara) and has few followers left.

Kusha: introduced by Chi-tsu in 660 and based on the Chü-she school, founded in China in 563 and itself derived from the third-century Indian school of Sarvastivadin. Died out in the Kamakura period.

Jojitsu: introduced by the Korean Dozo in 673, based on the Chinese Ch'êng shih school, which in turn derived from the Indian manual *Satya-siddhi* of Harivarman. Died out in the Kamakura period.

Kegon: founded by Roben in 740 after the Chinese Avatamska school. Chief temple: Todaiji in Nara.

Ritsu: introduced by the Chinese Ganjin (Chinese: Chien-chên) in 754, based on the 'School of Discipline' (*Lü-tsung*), which was founded in the 7th century by Tao-hsüan and which represents a combination of Hinayana and Mahayana. Chief temple: Toshodaiji in Nara. Few surviving followers.

XV *In May, on the occasion of the Tango-no-Sekku, the Festival of Boys and Children, which goes back to the Nara period, red and black flags are flown over the houses in the form of paper or cloth carps as symbols of manhood.*

Tendai: founded in 805 by Saicho, known by the posthumous name Dengyo-Daishi, after spending a year in China where he was a pupil of the Chih-chê. Emanating from the Chinese T'ien-t'ai school, though without its adherence to the Hinayana and incorporating elements of the Chinese Mantra school and of Shintoism. Main centre: Enryakuji on Mount Hiei near Kyoto. Two other branches have their head-quarters at Saikoji and Onjoji. This sect, which flourished in the 9th and 10th centuries, today has some 4,000 temples and 200,000 followers.

Shingon, the School of the True Word, was introduced in 806 by Kukai (774–835), posthumously known as Kobo Daishi, and is based on the Chinese 'School of Mysteries', which had emerged at the beginning of the 8th century from India through the Mahavairocana Sutra and the Susiddhikara Sutra. Main centre: Kongobuji, on Mount Koyasan; owns in Kyoto, inter alia, the temples of Toji, Daigoji and Sambo-in. The Sect flourished during the first half of the Heian Period and has today some 10,000 temples and a million followers.

The Reformed Shingon Sect *Shingi-shingon* was founded in 1132 by Kakuhan Shonin, known as Kokyo Daishi, and later split up into two branches, *Chizan* with its headquarters at Chishakuin (Kyoto), and *Buzan* with its headquarters in the temple of Hase.

THE AMIDA SECTS

Yuzu-nem-butsu, the Society for Mutual Welfare through Nembutsu (*i.e.* by repeated invocation of Amida with the words 'Namu Amida Budsu'), was founded in 1117 by the Tendai priest Ryonin, called Soo Daishi. Chief temple: Dainembutsuji in Osaka. Few surviving followers.

Jodo-shu, the School of the Pure Land, was founded by Genku or Honen (1133–1212), known as Enko Daishi, who belonged originally to the Tendai school. Main centre: Chion-in at Kyoto. Today more than 8,000 temples and some four million followers.

Three branches of this sect call themselves Jodo-Seizan and are adherents of Honen's pupil Shoku.

Shin-shu, the True Sect of the Pure Land, was founded by Shinran (1173–1262), a pupil of Honen, in 1201; their teaching is recorded in the Kyogyoshinsho script. Complete salvation can only come by the grace of Amida. This sect, which with some ten million followers is the most widespread of all, is split into two, one with its main centre at Higashi-Honganji (Kyoto) and over 10,000 temples, the other, older one with its centre at Nishi-Honganji (likewise Kyoto) and controlling some 9,500 temples.

Ji-shu, one of the smaller sects, was founded in 1276 by Ippen (1229–89). Main temple: Yugyoji in Fujisawa near Kamakura.

THE ZEN SECTS

Rinzai, founded by Eisai (1142–1215), author of Kozen Gokokuron, is based on the School of Meditation Ch'an-tsung, introduced into China by the Indian Bodhidharma, and the 'Theory of Suddenness' held

XVI *A woman gardener tending the trees in the garden of the Ginkakuji Temple (ill. 80) in Kyoto.*

by its southern adherents. The most important reformer: Hakuin (1685–1768). Today some two million followers. Of the 5,880 temples a few became centres of particular branches, for example in Kyoto: Nanzenji, Kenninji, Myoshinji, Tenruyji, and in Kamakura: Engakuji and Kenchoji.

Soto, founded in 1227 by Dogen (1220–52), author of Shobogenzo, based on the Chinese Ts'ao-tung school. Main temples Eiheiji and Sojiji at Tsurumi near Tokyo. Today about one and a half million followers with more than 14,000 temples.

Obaku, founded in 1654 by the Chinese priest Yin-yüan (Japanese: Ingen), based on the Chinese Huang-po school. The founder's successors as patriarchs were, for a long time, also Chinese. Main centre: Mampukuji at Uji (Kyoto).

NICHIREN AND THE LOTUS SECTS

Nichiren or *Hokke-shu*, *i.e.* Flower of the Law, founded in 1253 by Nichiren (1222–82), author of Rissho Ankokuron, an extension of the Tendai school. 'Namu Myoho renge-kyo' (Honour the Sutra of the Lotus of Truth). Main centre: Kuonji on Mount Minubu. More than 5,000 temples.

Nichiren-shoshu broke away at an early stage from Nichiren-shu under Nikko as the sole elected of Nichiren's six disciples. The doctrine was revived by Nikkan (1665–1726), the 26th Abbot of the Taisekji. The movement looks upon the historical Buddha as the forerunner of Nichiren, who is the Jogyo Bosatsu or Buddha of the Latter Day. It claims to possess the only genuine Nichiren relics and proclaims the 'three great secret laws': Daimoku, Honzon and Kaidan. The term Nichiren-shoshu only dates back to 1912.

Reiya-kai, the Society of Friends of the Soul, emerged in 1925 as a typical lay movement following the tragedy of the great 1923 earthquake, led by Kubo Kakutaro (1892–1940), his brother Kotami Yasukichi (1884–1929) and his brother's wife Mrs Kotani Kimi (born 1901). The movement combines worship of the Lotus Sutra with ancestor-worship and has specialized in social work; in 1940 it already had over a million followers, by 1960 3.7 million. The parent organization has engendered fifteen breakaway movements.

Soka-gakkai, Value Creating Society. The primary-school teacher Makiguchi Tsunesaburo (1871–1944), who was converted to the Nichiren school, formed a Society in 1937 for the dissemination of his 'Theory of Value'. After his death in prison the movement took on a new lease of life in 1946 under his friend Toda Josei (1900–58) and by 1961 had attracted over five million adherents. Since 1964 it has been represented in the local and national parliaments by the Komeito Party.

Rissho-Kosei-kai, the Society for the Establishment of Law and the Community, was founded in March 1938 as a lay missionary movement of 30 people and, in the political context of that period, described itself as 'pan-Japanese' (Dainippon). The founder was Naganuma Masa (1889–1957), who later called herself Myoko (Unique Humanity); her co-founder Niwano Shikzo (born 1906) adopted the name Nikkyo. Basic principle: 'To endeavour to do good; to try to become a Buddha of friendly disposition: that is what Nichiren wanted.' By 1961 the movement had two and a half million followers.

How was Christianity received in this strange world? Such is the readiness of the Japanese to interest themselves in anything new that contact with Western civilization, as was previously the case with the culture of China, was bound to arouse their curiosity about the religion of the new teachers. And this was, at least at first, what seemed to happen.

In 1532 Portuguese merchants landed for the first time on a Japanese island. They brought the first fire-arms into the country and the first Jesuit missionaries were not far behind. In 1549 St Francis Xavier, friend of Ignatius Loyola and the apostle of India, came to Kagoshima. His remarkable success in gaining converts embraced all strata of society. At times he was so successful that a Japanese could be baptized on the same day that he had first heard of the new teaching. Eleven of the daimyos of the south-west, including some of the most powerful territorial princes, entered the Catholic Church and by 1581 there were no less than 200-odd Jesuit churches, mainly on Kyushu. When the movement reached its peak towards the end of the 16th century, there were said to be between half a million and a million Catholic Christians in Japan, and conversions were even taking place in Kyoto, the ancient imperial capital.

But a reaction set in when the nation began to feel that its very foundations were being undermined. For the Christians were not prepared, as the Buddhists had been, to become part of the ancient destiny of the 'Land of the Gods'. They wanted to be sole arbiters of their destiny. They had no time for the 'idolatry' of the Shinto; Buddhist temples were burnt down and their priests killed. Financial donations spurred on conversion and certain feudal lords were doubtless friendly with the Jesuits because they were able to lay their hands on the coveted fire-arms. Portuguese merchants used the same ships to bring in the missionaries as they used to export Japanese for sale elsewhere as slaves. And the image of the Christians was not exactly improved by the fact that, once the Franciscans and Dominicans had appeared on the scene, the three missionary orders made no secret of their rivalry. And through the Dutch, whose trading ships were out to beat the Portuguese, it became known in Japan what methods the Inquisition was employing in Europe to deal with dissenters.

Each of the Three Great Unifiers of Japan, Nobunaga, Hideyoshi and Ieyasu, found himself compelled to change his initially tolerant attitude towards the Christians. In 1587 Hideyoshi issued a decree banishing the Jesuits and on 5th February 1597 six Spanish missionaries and twenty native Catholics were crucified in Nagasaki. Ieyasu, who, to begin with, had allowed the Christians to return to Kyoto and Osaka, was responsible for the ban imposed by his successor in 1614 and in 1637–38 when a violent uprising by the largely Christian population of Shimabara was only suppressed with great difficulty, the bakufu of Edo imposed a rigorous ban on Christians throughout the country and cut Japan off from the outside world.

That the Catholic missions had gained a firm footing in Japan became clear during the Meiji period when Christian worship was again permitted and several Christian communities which had been carrying on their worship in secret for over two hundred years emerged in Kyushu.

With the opening of Japan's doors, European and American Protestants entered into lively competition with the powerful Catholic Orders, but all the foreign missionaries soon found themselves competing with the Japanese Christians themselves, whose natural inclination to form sects began to reveal itself. The prayer-meetings of an English school engendered the Japan Christian Church, and in 1876 the Kumamoto Society of young Japanese was formed, which rejected any form of patronage by the missions. Somewhat later Uchimura Kanzo (1861–1930) became the leader of a movement which took the Bible as its sole authority and which today includes members of the intellectual elite among the followers of its 'anti-church Christianity'.

The Education Edict of 1890 and above all the militant nationalism of the nineteen-thirties attempted once again to discredit Christianity as an alien body but it had already become an ineradicable part of

Japanese life, and since 1945 the last barriers to its further dissemination have disappeared. The contribution of the Japanese Christians with their Universities, publishing-houses and social institutions is today a vital factor in Japan's national life. On the other hand, the landslide which might have been expected to follow on the successes of the 16th century did not materialize and the proportion of Christians in the Japanese population has never been more than, at the outside, one per cent.

The masses feel drawn to other, partly new faiths, whose apostles draw their strength from the deep well of ancient Shamanism and in the technological age have unleashed religious movements of elemental power. Some, as we have seen, look to their national prophet Nichiren, while others build their temples outside the jurisdiction of the traditional denominations. A brief survey of the most important of these 'modern religions' in Japan may serve to show how restless the Japanese are and how anxious, in their own individual way, to dedicate their lives to the service of an idea that transcends material things:

MODERN MOVEMENTS NOT ASSOCIATED WITH THE TRADITIONAL RELIGIONS:

Tenri-kyo, loosely classified in the beginning as a Shinto sect, was founded by Mrs Nakayama Miki (1798–1887). The revelations vouchsafed her from 1837 onwards were recorded in 1869–82 in a book entitled 'Truth of the Eternal Protection of the Founder'. The movement worships Oya-gami (Kami of elders) as Tenri-O-no-Mikoto (royal deity of divine reason). In the main, two forms of dance go to make up the service. Centre of the cult is the village of Tenri, which has grown into the town of Oyasako (Abode of the Elders). Today it has more than two million followers with over 100,000 priests and 15,000 temples.

Omoto-kyo was founded by Mrs Daguchi Nao (1836–1918). In the village of Ayabe she was 'possessed by God' in 1892 and began to preach. In 1898 she was joined by Ueda Kisaburo (1871–1948), who adopted the name Deguchi Onisaburo and since 1917 has been disseminating the writings of the founder. The doctrine centres around Omoto, *i.e.* first cause, great foundation. The Shinto god of storms combines with Miroku-Butsu (Maitreya), the Buddhist Messiah, to become the Saviour through whom the world becomes reconciled with God. Onisaburo also involved himself in worldly affairs; in 1924 he tried to raise an army in Mongolia to found a kingdom of peace, in 1929 he celebrated the Great Festival of World Reformation and he was frequently arrested. (In 1921 the first, and in 1935 the second 'Omoto incident'.) In 1952 the shrine was re-established at Ayabe.

Seicho-no-Ie proclaims the 'Fire of Growth' (Seicho). The movement dates back to the periodical of that name, published since 1930 by Tanaguchi Masaharu (born 1893), who is also a frequent broadcaster, who joined the Omoto movement briefly in 1917 and who has been influenced by Hegel, Bergson, Freud, Christian Science, etc. The movement which acquired legal status in 1949 has one and a half million followers.

Sekai Kyuseikyo was founded by Mokichi Okada (1882–1955), who came in contact with the Omoto movement in 1923. In 1926 he had his first revelation when the Kannon Sama took possession of his body. In 1934 he broke away from the Omoto movement and worked as a healer, regardless of official bans. In 1947 he revived his religious society, which adopted its present title in 1950. The main shrine is in Atami. The founder was succeeded as head of the movement in 1955 by his widow Nidaisama and in 1962 by her daughter Itsuki Fujieda.

PL-Kyodan, the Order of Perfect Liberty (PL-Perfect Liberty), was founded by Miki Tokuharu (1871–1938), who was trained as a Zen monk. He founded the Order after a meeting with the healer Kanada Tokumitsu (1863–1919), who was venerated as Daikyo-shi (Great True Teacher). He set up the Tokumitsu Church in Osaka. In 1924 he and 47 disciples formed a new community in the Ise shrine, which later became the *Hito no Michi* (Way of Man), and in 1931 the *Hito no Michi Kyodan* (Order of the Way of Man). The first meeting-place was in Tokyo and by 1931 the movement had a million followers. The Order preaches joyful living and, as it has encouraged the playing of golf, has also been called the 'Golf religion'.

Odoru Shukyo was founded by a peasant-woman, Kitamura Sayo (born 1900), the 'Prophetess of Tabuse': 'On 4 May 1944 God spoke to me for the first time.' On 12 August 1945 she was 'adopted as the only daughter of the absolute God of the universe' and after the war her preaching attracted more and more people. Frequently her sermons are followed by ecstatic dances as an expression of joy.

Ieyasu and the Tokugawa Dynasty

Of the three Unifiers of Japan, the first—the magnanimous Daimyo Oda Nobunaga—was assassinated by a traitorous general. The second—the meteoric genius Toyotomi Hideyoshi—was succeeded on his insecure throne by a minor, whereas his rival Tokugawa founded a dynasty of fifteen shoguns, which proved to be by far the most stable regime Japanese history had experienced until then.

In 1603, five years after Hideyoshi's death, Ieyasu had himself raised to the rank of shogun by the Tenno and only two years later he handed it on to his son Hidedata, although as Ogosho (abdicated shogun) he continued to control the State's affairs from his private seat at Sumpu until his death in 1616. He also saw to it that the power of the Toyotomi was finally broken in 1615, when the great fortress of Osaka was stormed, though at a heavy cost in human lives.

Ieyasu was no more scrupulous in the means he chose to seize power than other great men of history. He combined cunning and treachery with brilliant generalship, and human lives were not spared. On the other hand, where the interests of the State as he saw them did not call for severe measures, he proved to be a prudent ruler, who above all had the welfare of the ordinary man at heart. An Englishman, Will Adams, who came to Japan on board a Dutch ship, gave a detailed description of his journey to Edo and his audience with this outstanding man whom Europeans in general regarded as the 'Emperor', while the Tenno in Kyoto was looked upon as a mere spiritual overlord. To begin with, Adams was treated as a prisoner. Ieyasu questioned him at length about conditions in Europe and was so impressed by his honesty that he finally granted him the rank of samurai.

Under Ieyasu all the traditions Japan had acquired since Shotoku Taishi were fused into one living organism and in the Tokugawa period a highly disciplined nation emerged, which was to survive all the storms of the twentieth century. After his death the first Tokugawa shogun was accorded the highest honours ever bestowed on a Japanese: he was made a god. Over his grave at Nikko a shrine of ostentatious splendour was erected with an imperial prince as chief priest.

Ieyasu did not create a new system of government but he did succeed in achieving an effective balance of power between the central authority and the regions. The predominance of the shogun in Edo was assured by his vast domain, which was administered by his feudal tenants. His territory included the most important towns, such as Kyoto, Osaka and Nagasaki, and the richest mines. The remainder of the country was divided up into the greater or lesser principalities of the daimyos. These territorial over-lords continued to enjoy a large measure of autonomy but, as they spent half the year—more or less voluntarily—in Edo and when they returned to their castles they left their families behind as hostages, they were constantly and effectively supervised. The shogun was the arbiter in any quarrels between the daimyos; he could fill or merge vacant daimyats, and during the Tokugawa period the number of dai-myats varied accordingly from 245 to 295.

In the rigidly hierarchical society of Ieyasu's time the principles of Confucianism were restored to favour. The higher the rank, the stricter the moral obligations, while the mass of the people enjoyed a fair degree of tolerance. In each stratum of society the basic unit was the family or rather the greater family, the clan, to which the individual adapted and subordinated himself as a matter of course. The individual rights which evolved in the European period of the Enlightenment remained alien to the Japanese until quite recently. Of the four classical Estates the warriors or samurai occupied the highest position; the peasants came next, then the artisans, and the merchants had to be content with the lowest status.

The laws which varied from daimyat to daimyat governed the life of the community down to the smallest detail. The exact size and type of roof on a peasant's house was prescribed in accordance with the amount of rice he produced. The kind of food provided at weddings, the presents given and the clothes worn on ceremonial occasions were all predetermined by social status and by income. The peasant always left his door unlocked in order not to offend his fellow villagers. Entry into the priesthood required official approval.

The samurai paid for his privileged position with the rigorous code of honour of the Bushido. Even a relatively minor deviation from the code was enough to require ritual suicide by *harakiri* (slitting open the stomach, usually accompanied by decapitation by a friend), or, to employ the more distinguished Chinese term, *seppuku*. But *seppuku* was also sometimes committed by blameless knights merely as a form of moral protest or to keep the nation alive to the spirit of unconditional loyalty. In 1912, for example, General Nogi, the hero of the Russo-Japanese war, and his wife committed *seppuku* on the day the Emperor Meiji was buried.

The Tokugawa empire was in its way a police State but it was also something more. Five main roads linked Edo with the provinces, trade prospered during a prolonged period of peace, standards of living improved, and in the courts of Kyoto and Edo as well as in the many monasteries the arts and sciences were actively cultivated. There was a marked growth in interest in the arts, which was particularly apparent in the magnificent woodcuts and in the development of the theatre, and which show how the less mate-rialistic side of life was made available to an increasingly wide cross-section of society.

Like Shotoku Taishi in his seventeen articles a thousand years before, Ieyasu also left a kind of political testament, which is not confined, however, to general principles but also deals with day-to-day problems. It is therefore more a product of the age in which it was written and gives a realistic insight into contemporary Japan.

A year before he died Ieyasu issued eighteen laws, seventeen of which have survived in garbled form. The first law is concerned with the significance of the imperial house; a free rendering would run much as follows: 'According to an ancient teaching of the land of the gods, the gods are the spirits of heaven, the emperors those of the earth. The treasures handed down from the time of the gods help the Son of Heaven to nourish and educate all peoples between the four seas. The Tenno shall keep his sublime heart untouched. Every day he shall pray to heaven that through humanity, love of parents, perspicacity and frugality he may shine forth as an example to the land. In the cultivation of the sciences and the art of writing he shall also not be negligent ...'

The second law defines the position of the shogun: 'Since the office of a Betto of Djunna and Sogaku-In was transferred to the shogun of Kanto, the three Shinno (the princes designated to perpetuate the imperial house), the sekke, kuge and daimyos are all subject to the latter. By his orders he administers all affairs of State and in government matters does not require the approval of the Tenno.'

In the other articles it is twice pointed out that the omnipotence of the shogun must be dependent on his own performance, for 'if the shogun behaves despotically and ruthlessly and fills the people with sorrow', one of the two daimyos designated for that purpose will be chosen to succeed him and proposed to the Tenno.

The predominance of the samurai is based on the assertion that, 'because the kuge (court nobility) were weak in government and were unable to maintain order in the land, the only course left open was for the buke (military nobility) to receive orders from the Tenno for them to take over the ancient government.'

Also worth noting is the explanation why the Tenno should not in future leave his palace in Kyoto: 'In ancient times the emperors were wont to make the pilgrimage to Kumano in Ise to Shinto and Buddhist temples, and this they did in order that they might become familiar on their way with the sufferings of the people. But now the Tenno has reformed the government and entrusted it to the military nobility. If they are not aware of the sufferings of the people, then the fault lies with the shogun.'

The remaining laws define the jurisdiction of individual offices, including those of the priesthood, and deal with questions of succession. Referring to the ancient foundations of the Japanese State, Ieyasu also delivers a brief homily on the purpose of laws in general: 'The decrees issued by Yoritomo Minamoto and the Seventeen Articles of Shotoku must form the basis of future legislation. The laws are the justice of heaven and of earth. If they are in keeping with the spirit of the times and if justice is clearly reflected in them, then the people will accept them and they will have the effect of keeping heaven and earth in harmony with one another. If, however, they offend against (natural) justice, then the people will fail to observe them.'

To Ieyasu are also ascribed another hundred 'laws' as a political testament, in which he expressed his views on many theoretical and practical problems. Here are a few examples to round off our picture of the Tokugawa period:

ARTICLE 16
That I fought against my country's enemies from my early youth came about solely in order that I might take my revenge on my father's adversaries. And because I was convinced of the rightness of my intention to help the people and bring peace to the land in accordance with the teaching of (the priest) Yuyo, I was successful. My descendants must therefore continue to act in the same spirit.

ARTICLE 23
There is an old saying: 'Even if all those around you advise you to kill this or that man, do not listen. But if the people say, kill this or that man, then consider if this is right and then kill him. And if all those around you say, reward him, then do not listen. But if the people say, reward him, then consider if this is right and

then reward him.' This saying contains all the art of government and those who act in defiance of it must know that they are destroying their own gods and their country.

ARTICLE 25

Song and music are not the main occupation of the shoguns, but at certain times they lighten the troubled spirit and make the joys of peace even more pleasant.

ARTICLE 29

High and low may subscribe to any of the old established religions, with the exception of the *abominable* (? Christian) religion. Since time immemorial religious strife has brought disaster to the world. One must therefore see to it that it ceases altogether.

ARTICLE 44

Any man who has passed his sixteenth year should no longer live alone, but seek a marriage-suitor ...

ARTICLE 45

Any man who has no son should adopt a child ...

ARTICLE 52

The same distinction should hold good between wife and concubine as between master and servant. The Emperor has twelve concubines, the princes have eight, the taifu five and the samurai two. All persons of lower rank have only one wedded wife. So have the old wise men in the book Raiki ordained and so it has been since ancient times. Blockheads who do not understand this custom and who in passionate love for the concubines neglect their wives, offend against the basic laws of human society. It is for this reason that so many castles fell and so many countries were ruined in ancient times. Must one not intervene with a warning? He who is deep in lust cannot be a true vassal, that you must know in advance.

ARTICLE 53

The man looks after the affairs outside the house, the woman keeps order inside it, as custom requires everywhere under heaven.

ARTICLE 70

Master and servant should be as well suited to one another as water and fish, says an old proverb, and this is not hard to achieve. He who always keeps in his heart the golden words, 'What you do not like,

XVII *The Golden Pavilion, one of the most famous monuments of the Muromachi period, after which the Kinkakuji Temple at Kyoto is named, was damaged by fire in 1950 and was restored in its full gilded glory in 1955. The third Ashikaga shogun, Yoshimitsu, after retiring from his official position in 1394, had built himself a splendid country residence at the foot of Mount Kinugasa; in accordance with his last will and testament, under his successor Yoshimochi the building was converted into the Rokuonji Temple of the Rinzai sect of Zen, sub-sect Shoku-ji.*

XVIII *The buildings of the Nishi-Honganji at Kyoto (ill. 75), chief temple of the older branch of the Shin sect, are particularly rich in examples of the magnificent interior decoration of temples and palaces during the Momoyama and early Edo periods. The corridor before the Audience Hall was decorated by Kaihoku Yusetsu (1598–1677), one of the masters of the Kano school, who painted partially opened books on the ceiling and wistarias on the wall.*

do not inflict upon others,' will find his servants like to him in virtue. But not to the servants alone, this virtue must spread like a stream to the very lowest.

ARTICLE 71

We, like all others, have received our bodies from the land of the gods. But while in the various provinces of the empire the teachings of the philosophers (Confucius, etc.), of the Shakka (Buddha), of the Sendo (Way of the Contemplative Life) and others are revered by the people, the Kami religion (Shinto) is neglected. This, I think, is just as if one were to quarrel with one's master and transfer one's loyalty to a strange master, and the foundation is thereby destroyed. Among the named sects you should choose exactly which you must esteem and which you must reject. All sects that concern themselves with magic and secret acts you should not love, yet you should not push them violently aside.

ARTICLE 74

Prostitutes and females who make mischief on the streets at night are like the insects that infest any country; they are, as the wise man (Confucius) mentions in many writings and laws, a necessary evil. If one were to take stern measures against them, then public order would merely be disturbed, and the contraventions would be so numerous that it would be impossible to punish all of them. Towards the small offences of the common people, one should, as the Chinese Emperor Kooso has done, show indulgence and charity.

ARTICLE 76

If the power of the buke (the military nobility) becomes too great, respect for the emperor declines. This has always been so. But the foundations of the land of the gods are thereby destroyed and selfishness and despotism reach their peak. This is therefore no small crime and will surely bring down the punishment of heaven.

ARTICLE 94

When envoys from foreign lands come here bearing gifts, they should be splendidly entertained, the forms of courtesy carefully observed and military equipment be scrupulously clean. From the port where the foreign ship has dropped anchor to Edo, the castles, walls and houses on the routes, both in our own and foreign regions, should be most carefully repaired and care should be taken to display the prosperity, wealth and military efficiency of the Empire.

ARTICLE 95

When strangers arrive unannounced at our shores in their ships from the remote foreign islands, this should immediately be reported here and the interpreters should ascertain by written exchange what is the purpose of their coming. Accordingly, one should thereupon treat them in a friendly or a very severe fashion. One should place watches over them and not pursue any trade with them.

The Meiji Reforms

In the spring of 1869 when the sixteen-year-old Emperor Mutsuhito travelled in solemn procession from Kyoto, which had been the residence of his forefathers for a thousand years, eastwards to Edo in order to move into the castle of the imperial regent, who had retired, not only a new nengo with the promising name of Meiji (Enlightened Government) had appeared but a new age had dawned for Japan. The island-empire emerged from its hermetic isolation, faced up to the problems of the age and set out to play its part in the world-wide competition between the technologically advanced nations. With the departure of the last shogun, the tough reactionary forces of the medieval period seemed to abdicate and the appearance of the young Tenno, his full authority once again restored to him, seemed to mark a victory for the forces of progress. But the subsequent course of events and the part played by the leading personalities do not present quite such a simple picture.

Since the establishment of the bakufu of Edo, the population of Japan had grown from about fifteen million to double that figure. In the long period of peace industry and trade had prospered and, thanks to efficient cultivation of the soil, the increased demand for food had been met. There was hardly any trace of social unrest. The standard of education of the people was extraordinarily high, as can be seen from a paragraph in Meyer's *Conversationslexicon* of 1850: 'The education of the children, which is entirely adapted to the ceremonial life of the Japanese, is strict and of its kind outstanding. With their 7th year the instruction of boys and girls begins at public schools, where reading, writing, arithmetic and national history are taught, so that as a rule the meanest of wage-earners has this knowledge.'

But after 250 years even the most vigorous system shows signs of exhaustion. The feudal lords, above all the powerful daimyos of Choshu and Satsuma, who had been kept so long in check, were merely ideological discussions waiting for an opportunity to shake off the yoke of the Tokugawa; the became more heated in intellectual circles, but more acute was the growing pressure from other countries to penetrate this closed land with something more solid than mere ideas.

In July 1853 Commodore Perry sailed into the Bay of Edo with four United States warships and demanded that Japanese ports be opened to trade with America. He was fobbed off with the promise of an answer next year. On his return with a larger fleet a few salvoes from his guns were enough to set negotiations in train. As, apart from the Chinese, the Dutch were the only foreigners who had been allowed to trade with Japan since the 16th century, the negotiations were conducted, and an agreement was reached, in Dutch. On 31 March 1854 the first 'Treaty of Friendship' was signed at Kanagawa (Yokohama), and the Americans set the seal on the agreement by making symbolic gifts of a railway with steam-engine and an electric telegraph. Immediately after the first American visit to Edo, seven Russian ships appeared at Nagasaki and agreements were also concluded with Tsarist Russia, Great Britain and the Netherlands.

In authoritative circles in Japan, including the daimyos, the supporters and the opponents of these agreements with the foreigners were more or less evenly balanced. The leader of the opposition was the reactionary Tenno Komei (1846–66). Behind him were ranged all those whose motto was: *Son-no, jo-i!* (Honour the Emperor, drive out the foreigner!)

In 1858 the daimyo of Hikone, Ii Naosuko, took over as *tairo* control of the bakufu at Edo; in the same year (on 29 July) he brought the negotiations with the American Consul General Townsend Harris for a trade agreement to a successful conclusion. Shortly afterwards Lord Elgin obtained similar concessions for England (26 August), and France was represented in Edo by a Consul General.

One of the first European nations to try to establish trading relations was Switzerland, under strong pressure from the watch industry, but its first delegation in 1859 was informed that, 'owing to shortage of means of production and of foodstuffs', Japan could not extend her trade to any other countries. But the Swiss were promised that they would not lose their place in the queue.

Ii Naosuko, who appointed Ieshige, a minor, to succeed the late shogun and who ruthlessly suppressed opposition to the treaties, was assassinated on 3 March 1860 by one of the young 'determined men', the *shishi*, who emerged as champions of a nationalist movement. Following in the footsteps of the roving bands of samurai freebooters, whose exploits and heroic deeds have been immortalized in so many stories, they proceeded over the next few decades to execute a whole series of ministers; they revolted as officers against their weaker leaders; they were the *kamikaze* (Wind of the Gods) who plunged with their bomb-loads on enemy warships in the Second World War, and after the catastrophe of Hiroshima shrank from nothing to try and prevent the capitulation.

The course of events was by now well set. In August 1860 Portugal, the first of Japan's trading partners, was re-admitted. A month later Count Friedrich zu Eulenburg appeared with a Prussian naval squadron and, after protracted negotiations, a treaty was concluded on 21 January 1861. Switzerland's special envoy, Aimé Hubert, signed the first trade agreement between his country and Japan, and other States followed.

In the meantime the conflict between Japan's leaders was coming to a head. In 1863 the shogun went to Kyoto to obtain the Tenno's sanction for the treaties, but the latter, encouraged by the revival of imperial authority, gave orders for the foreigners to be expelled, one and all. The bakufu was now caught between the Emperor, supported by the xenophobic daimyos, and the foreign warships with their superior weapons.

The burning-down of foreign legations at Edo, the murder of an Englishman and the molestation of Western warships by the coastal batteries at Satsuma and Choshu resulted in the bombardment of Kago-shima and Shimonoseki. For the time being at least, the point was taken: the daimyos of Choshu and Satsuma recruited English instructors, while the shogun brought in Frenchmen to reorganize his army. Choshu rebelled openly against the central government in Edo, and the two punitive expeditions organized by the bakufu failed to suppress the rebellion.

The death of the shogun Ieshige, who was still a young man, and in the same year, 1866, of the Emperor Komei left the two highest positions in the State vacant. Yoshinubu from the Mito branch of the Tokugawa, reluctant to take office, tried to introduce reforms. This last of the shoguns declared himself in favour of a redistribution of power and was even prepared to facilitate the process by abdicating. All that stood in the way of a united country under the sole rule of the Tenno was the opposition among the followers of the Tokugawa.

In January 1867 Mutsuhito, then 15 years of age, succeeded his late father as emperor. The young Tenno's supporters, who were to be the architects of the Meiji period, were drawn from the traditional court nobility, the daimyos and their followers, and the samurai. Among the outstanding statesmen of the new Japan the representatives of the Satsuma and Choshu families, traditional enemies of the Tokugawa, were particularly prominent. The leading figure among the first imperial ministers, Okubo Tosimiki was a Satsuma man, while the brilliant Choshu general, Omura Masujiro (assassinated in 1869), became head of the newly-created War Ministry. Also from Choshu were Ito Hirobumi (1841–1901), the first Prime Minister, Yamagata Aritomo (1838–1922), the first Minister of the Interior and later Prime Minister, and Inoue Kaoru (1835–1915), the first Foreign Minister, while two of the Prime Ministers, Kuroda Kiyotaka (1840–1900) and Matsukata Masayoshi (1837–1924), were from Satsuma.

The basic principles underlying the State reforms which were solemnly proclaimed by the Tenno culminated in the following demand: 'Knowledge must be acquired from all parts of the world and the interests of the Imperial State thereby fundamentally promoted.' In place of the old xenophobic imperial watchword a new motto was coined: 'Enrich the State and strengthen the fighting forces!' (Fukoku-kyohei).

Leading personalities travelled abroad and gained their first insight into the machinery of a modern industrial state. A veritable hurricane of reforms swept through the ancient imperial edifice, shaking it to its foundations. With extraordinary energy the Japanese nation set about converting itself from an underdeveloped country into a modern Great Power.

The Tokugawa estates were confiscated by the State and as early as 1869 the daimyos also placed their principalities at the disposal of the Emperor, in order to promote the cause of national unity. There had been a precedent in the Nara period, when an attempt was made to establish an imperial system based on the Chinese model. To begin with, the feudal overlords were given posts as governors in their former domains, but before long a more rational distribution of the Empire into prefectures was introduced. The year 1873 brought not only a far-reaching reform of the tax system but also the introduction of conscription. The samurai, who numbered about 400,000 and whose role as a privileged caste of warriors was abolished, were given financial compensation and obliged to seek civilian employment, although many found their way into the police. There were revolts at Saga (1874), Kumamoto (1876) and Kagoshima (1877) but all three were crushed and there was no further serious resistance to the reforms. As private undertakings with sufficient capital did not exist, the government itself had to take the initiative in stimulating industrialization but plants were sold as soon as possible to private enterprise. From the old ruling class a new oligarchy of politicians and industrialists emerged, which again was based on groups of kinship. In the ideological struggle that followed the principal forces involved were the liberalism of England and France, the militarism of the Prussian junkers, the philosophy of Spencer, Darwinism, and the reform movements among the Buddhist sects and in State Shintoism, to say nothing of the socialist mass-movements which were already looming up on the horizon.

The first major achievement of the Meiji reforms was the 'Great Japanese Imperial Constitution' (Dainihon Teikoku Kempo) of 1889. Closely modelled on the conservative Prussian Constitution, it still remained essentially Japanese; as John Whitney Hall has pointed out, it 'retains the peculiar form in which the Japanese reached their political decisions and which left undisclosed who was the responsible man behind a "not responsible sovereign", who voiced the concensus of opinion of his political advisers.'

Marquis Ito Hirobumi, who drew up the Constitution and took over the reins of government four times, describes the aims of the Meiji reformers in his contribution to *Japan by the Japanese* edited by Alfred Stead (London 1904):

'I was one of the first Japanese to visit foreign lands, and was only able to do so by stealth, escaping to Shanghai in 1863. The country was only just opened to foreign intercourse, and Japanese subjects were not yet allowed to leave the country.

'I have always been very much in favour of the adoption of the principles of Western civilization by Japan, and I have been enabled to use my services in the direction of assisting the present progress and transformation in Japan's estate. In the thirty-four years during which I have held office I have always tried to help, and sometimes even to force on to the antagonistic spirits, measures necessary for the growth of modern

Japan. From the beginning we realized fully how necessary it was that the Japanese people should not only adopt Western methods, but should also speedily become competent to do without the aid of foreign instruction and supervision. In the early days we brought many foreigners to Japan to help to introduce modern methods, but we always did it in such a way as to enable the Japanese students to take their rightful place in the nation after they had been educated . . . .

'On the occasion of my second visit to London as one of the Ambassadors of our country, it was suggested to me that it would be most beneficial to establish a special Engineering College in Japan, where every branch of engineering should be taught. Such a college would be quite unique, no other nation having one. The idea seemed a very good one, and on my return to Japan I took the necessary steps, and with the assistance of foreign professors we founded an Engineering College, now incorporated in the Tokyo University. From this institution have come the majority of engineers who are now working the resources and industries of Japan. I consider the establishment of this college as one of the most important factors in the development of Japan to-day.

'It was most necessary that Japan should not only be educated, but also provided with suitable codes of laws, before there could be any question of a revision of the treaties with foreign nations, and for a considerable time all our efforts were turned in this direction.

'There are two events in Japanese history that have been all-important. The first was the change of regime of government of the country and the promulgation of the Constitution, and the other was the Sino-Japanese War. I spent much time away from Japan studying the Constitutions of various countries, the Emperor having ordered me to undertake the arduous task of framing a draft of the new Japanese Constitution. The work was very difficult and necessitated much thought. Never before had there been a Constitution, in the modern sense of the word, in Japan, to help me to know what were the most vital points to be provided for in the new code. The country had been so essentially a non-constitutional and feudal one that it was difficult to sit down on the debris of its past history and prepare off-hand a Constitution for it. Above all, there was the pre-eminent importance to be attached to the necessity of safeguarding the sacred and traditional rights of the Sovereign.'

With the example of the other great island-nation, Great Britain, before it, the Japanese Empire set about finding foreign markets, sources of raw materials and development areas for its growing industry and rapidly increasing population. But by contrast with the British, for whom military power has always been merely a means to an end, the armed forces in the new Japanese colonial empire became the acknowledged champions of national tradition and eventually assumed sole leadership. As early as 1880 the new Imperial General Staff had asserted that both army and navy should be independent of the politicians and had made them directly responsible to the Tenno; this meant that they appointed the Ministries of War and Marine and occupied a key position in the government, which, when circumstances demanded it, they were prepared to exploit ruthlessly.

Without waiting for the 'one-sided' treaties which she had signed to be revoked (this did not happen until 1899), Japan confronted her weaker Asian neighbours with certain demands. In 1875 she forced the Koreans to open their ports and this was followed in 1882 by the stationing of two companies of troops at the legation in Seoul. In 1894 war was declared on the Chinese Empire following its intervention in Korea, Port Arthur was occupied and the Chinese fleet destroyed. In the Peace of Shimonoseki Japan acquired Formosa but, following protests by the Western powers, the Liaotung peninsula, which had also been occupied, had to be evacuated. In 1900, during the Boxer Rebellion, the Japanese took part in the occupation of Peking and their troops made an impressive showing. The alliance with Great Britain concluded in 1902 meant that the empire in the Far East had been accepted as a full member of the Great Powers' club.

On 18 February 1904 war was declared on the great continental colonial power, Russia, which was also exploiting China's weakness and pushing forward through Manchuria towards the Pacific. The following year the powerful Czarist empire, beaten both at sea and on land, had to sign the Treaty of Portsmouth with the Americans acting as mediators. In 1910 Korea was annexed. In 1914 Japan fulfilled her obligation under the alliance with Britain and entered the war against Germany, occupying her Chinese possession Tsingtau. On 18 January Japan presented the young Chinese republic, which was without any established central government, with the famous 21 Demands. In 1921 the Japanese felt strong enough to allow the alliance with Britain to expire.

In 1922 the return of Tsingtau to China seemed to pave the way for better relations. At home the political parties were beginning to put forward demands for a more liberal regime and the factory-workers, under the impetus of the Russian Revolution, were becoming aware of their organized power. But amongst the young officers socialist ideas were combined with an ultra-nationalism which aimed at eventual world-domination. There was a growing demand for the abolition of the outmoded Meiji reforms and for the Showa Restoration, so-called after the reign of the Emperor Hirohito, who succeeded to the throne in 1926.

With the 'Manchurian Incident' in 1931 the army took effective control, for the commandant of the Kwantung army, which patrolled the Manchurian railway, ignored the instructions of the Tokyo government and opened hostilities with China. In May 1932 came the first attempt to overthrow the government and implement the Showa Restoration, and Prime Minister Inukai was assassinated in Tokyo. The much more dangerous and bloody officers' revolt in February 1936 was only suppressed when the Tenno intervened personally against the rebels. But the failure of the fanatical spearhead did not appreciably weaken the nationalist movement as such. In 1933 Japan left the League of Nations. Manchuria became a puppet-empire and was fully exploited.

In November 1936 the first 'anti-Communist' agreement was reached with Hitler, which later developed into the anti-Western Berlin–Rome–Tokyo Axis. On 7 July 1937, following an exchange of fire on the Marco Polo Bridge near Peking, the Japanese invaded China. Later that same year Nanking, seat of Chiang Kai-shek's national government, was occupied, and the following year the Japanese entered the southern capital, Canton. By the beginning of 1940 the political parties in Japan had lost all influence and they were replaced by the 'Association for the Promotion of the Imperial Dynasty' (Taisei Yokusankai). The Neutrality Pact of 1941 prepared the ground for the approaching clash with the Anglo-Saxon powers. In October of the same year General Tojo, the exponent of the military party, himself took over the reins of government and, while Japanese delegates were still negotiating in Washington, the Japanese airforce dealt its crushing blow to the American fleet in Pearl Harbor on 7 December 1941.

The Voice of the Cranes*

The cry of the crane, the imperial bird, echoes far across the sky. The voice of the crane in ancient times was the announcement of a fateful decision, which could only be made through the sacred mouth of the Tenno. Since the beginning of recorded time Japan had not heard the voice of the crane.

His Majesty Hirohito, the hundred and twenty-fourth of the Tennos to trace his descent back to the Land of the Gods, was burdened with the office of regent at the age of twenty, when his father was too ill to rule. This inconspicuous, modest man is surrounded by a wall of veneration. His people seldom see him—unless it be from a distance when he attends a parade mounted on his white horse—and even in the age of broadcasting his voice is never heard. Early in the morning he starts his day's work by paying his respects to his distinguished ancestors, then settles down at his writing-desk where busts of Charles Darwin and Abraham Lincoln look down on him. His views were not sought at the time of the Manchurian Incident or the invasion of China, nor when the attack on Pearl Harbor marked the first step towards world-domination. But everything happens in his name, involving his divine mission. Ministers are assassinated because they 'wrongly advised' His Imperial Majesty. But who decides what the correct advice is?

The war machine which was set in motion with the attack on Pearl Harbor fulfilled the boldest expectations: the Americans were driven out of the Philippines, the British out of Hong Kong and Singapore, the Dutch out of Indonesia, and British India was threatened from Burma. The establishment of a Japanese-dominated Asia seemed very close.

But the first reverse came in June 1942 at the naval battle of Midway Island. Before long the Japanese armaments industry was unable to meet the growing demands made on it, whereas the enemy's reserves were inexhaustible, and even the 'divine wind' of the suicide squadrons was unable to make much impression on the enemy's airforce. When Hitler's empire collapsed, Japan was also exhausted; from island to island she had to give up her spoils but continued to fight on grimly, while American bombers rained destruction on her cities. The death-toll was enormous: more than three million people lost their lives at the front or at home, of whom 800,000 were civilians.

On 26 July 1945 the victorious Allies meeting in Potsdam called on Japan to surrender. In their declaration they said:

*This account of the events connected with the imperial proclamation of 15 August 1945 with the dramatic turn of phrase so typical of the Japanese character and tradition is based on the book *Japan's Longest Day* (Kodausha International Ltd, Tokyo 1968) published by the Pacific War Research Society.

'We do not intend that the Japanese shall be enslaved as a race nor destroyed as a nation, but stern justice will be meted out to all war criminals, including those who have visited cruelties upon our prisoners. The Japanese Government shall remove all obstacles to the revival and strengthening of democratic tendencies among the Japanese people. Freedom of speech, of religion and of thought as well as respect for fundamental human rights shall be established...

'We call upon the Government of Japan to proclaim now the unconditional surrender of all the Japanese armed forces and to provide proper and adequate assurances of their good faith in such action. The alternative for Japan is complete and utter destruction.'

Foreign Minister Togo tried to convince his Cabinet colleagues that it was better to accept the Potsdam terms today rather than tomorrow. But War Minister Korechika Anami would not hear of capitulation. Had it not always been the Army's watchword that a Japanese never surrendered? His own people would regard him as a traitor if such a decision were taken and his whole Ministry would revolt against it. Not a single enemy soldier had so far set foot on the sacred soil of Japan and there was still hope that any invader would be repulsed with heavy losses.

The Prime Minister—it was no longer the firebrand Tojo but the cautious Baron Suzuki—hesitated. He knew that Foreign Minister Togo was right but he did not dare say so openly. On the radio he stated that the Potsdam Declaration was 'of no great value' and that Japan would fight on. The reply came on 6 August with the first atom bomb on Hiroshima. At the same time the 'normal' air-raids, which had already reduced Tokyo to a heap of ruins, continued without interruption. In despair the Foreign Minister tried to persuade Moscow, which was still nominally neutral, to act as mediator, but the Russians wanted to be sure of getting their share of the loot and marched into Manchuria.

Throughout the whole of 9 August the Supreme War Council and the Council of Ministers were in session. While their discussions were still going on, news came of the explosion of a second atom bomb, this time over Nagasaki. It was generally assumed that Tokyo with its enormous population would be the third target for this appalling weapon.

General Anami was now prepared to accept the Potsdam Declaration, albeit on certain conditions, but the Foreign Minister and with him the Head of Government knew from President Truman's latest statement that the time was past when conditions could be laid down. On one point, however, all were agreed: the position of the Emperor as Supreme Head of State must on no account be surrendered.

As the Council of War and the Cabinet were not unanimous on the Potsdam Declaration and a change of government would have involved a delay which in the circumstances was unthinkable, Baron Suzuki decided to take a step which had no precedent in Japan, namely not to submit to the Tenno for his formal sanction the usual unanimous decision of his advisers but to confront him with the dilemma of deciding himself.

Hirohito was not unprepared for this turn of events. As early as February 1942, when the entire world was aghast at Japan's victories, the Lord Keeper of the Privy Seal Kido, who enjoyed his confidence, impressed upon him the necessity of 'seizing the earliest opportunity to bring the war to an end as soon as possible'. On 9 August the Emperor was also in constant touch with Kido and he took the precaution of receiving the Director of the Department of Information, and, in the course of a long audience, declaring his readiness, should the need arise, to address the people personally on the radio.

At a late hour the Supreme War Council met in the air-raid shelter of the imperial library, serving as the imperial residence since the Meiji palace was destroyed. Around midnight Hirohito entered the small, stifling room. The leaders of the government, army and navy expressed their various conflicting views. And then the voice of the crane was heard: 'The moment has come to bear the unbearable... I give my approval to the acceptance of the proclamation by the Allied Powers on the basis outlined by the Foreign Minister.'

In the small hours the Council of Ministers, which alone could reach a final decision, met and early in the morning of 10 August a telegram was despatched to Switzerland and Sweden to be forwarded to the Allies. In it the Japanese Government accepted the Potsdam Declaration 'on the understanding that the said Declaration does not comprise any demand which prejudices the prerogatives of His Majesty as a Sovereign Ruler'.

XIX *Forming the background to the garden of Tentoku-in, one of the many monastery-temples in the vicinity of the great temple on Koyasan, are the tall trees of the surrounding forest.*

Later that morning General Anami appeared before the assembled staff of his Ministry, centre of a war-machine which was still extremely powerful. Everything now depended on whether the enemy would accept this one condition. The officers, who had always been prepared, if the situation demanded it, to ignore decisions of their 'wrongly advised' sovereign, were outraged. The War Minister reminded them coldly of their oath of obedience. 'Anyone who disregards my orders will do so over my dead body.'

In the White House in Washington the Japanese note was discussed. It was agreed that the authority of the Emperor would at least be required to complete the surrender. The Americans reached agreement with London and Moscow; the Russian demand that they should be represented at the occupation by a senior Soviet officer was rejected as 'absolutely unacceptable'. The reply of the Allied Powers was communicated to the Japanese on 11 August: 'From the moment of the surrender the authority of the Emperor and the Japanese Government to rule the State shall be subject to the Supreme Commander of the Allied Powers.'

In the meantime the Japanese had issued through the Press and the radio a statement that was as non-committal and indecisive as possible; but at the same time the all-powerful War Ministry, without consulting its chief, issued an appeal through the same media, calling upon the people to continue fighting, 'even if we have to chew grass and eat earth and sleep in the fields'. A plot was being hatched by the officers. Among those marked down for execution by the Resolute Men were Suzuki, Togo and Kido.

The Japanese are models of self-discipline. For centuries their leaders had been brought up in the belief that they must never spare themselves and must, if necessary, be prepared to commit seppuku, quite cold-bloodedly and with ritual precision. The example of General Nogi in 1945 was still fresh in their minds. Nobody was more alive to it than the War Minister, General Anami. But it is by no means inconsistent with this stern virility—as patrons of the Japanese theatre know from experience—that agonizing pain should not be concealed and tears should be allowed to flow. The Ministers and Generals who were fated to accept the first capitulation in Japan's long history kept wiping both sweat and tears from their faces. Admiral Onishi, the organizer of the Kamikaze Suicide Commandos, broke into heart-rending sobs when his superior, Navy Minister Yonei, took him to task for a contemptuous remark he had made. But no sooner had he recovered than he offered, during a discussion between defence chiefs and the Foreign Minister, to organize massive Kamikaze attacks which would mean sacrificing twenty million Japanese lives but which would turn the tide of war.

Was the answer of the Allies a Yes or a No to Japan's sole condition? In the Supreme War Council the Prime Minister, the Foreign Minister and the Navy Minister said Yes, the War Minister and the two Chiefs of Staff said No. The Cabinet was also divided and once again Suzuki appealed to 'the voice of the crane'.

XX *Near the village of Shugakuin at the foot of Mount Hiei to the north-east of Kyoto the abdicated Emperor Go-Mizuno-o built a country-seat where he could retire as a Zen monk and meditate. Three houses were built, each with a garden, which today form the imperial villa of Shugakuin. In the highest of the three gardens the shogun Ienari built the Chitose or Thousand Years Bridge in 1824 when the place was restored for the abdicated Emperor Kokaku.*

XXI *The 'Imperial Detached Palace' of Katsura to the south-west of Kyoto was originally a country residence and was extended in 1590 for the Imperial Prince Tomohito. Under Prince Toshihito, the first Duke of Hachijo, and his successor Toshitada the famous garden was created and is regarded as a masterpiece of Kobori Enshu (1579–1647), who was skilled in all the arts.*

On the morning of 14 August the Emperor summoned Field Marshals Hata and Sugiyama. He informed them of his decision to end the war and asked for their support. Then he descended to the air-raid shelter, where the entire Cabinet was assembled. The Prime Minister gave a sober account of the situation, from which it was clear that he saw no alternative but to accept immediately the allied conditions, even if, on the all-important question of the Emperor, they were, to say the least, unclear. But, at the same time, they were not a clear negative. The other members of the Cabinet cast their conflicting votes, each stating his case with the utmost inner conviction. Finally all eyes turned respectfully to the bespectacled figure in plain uniform seated alone at a small table in front of the golden screen.

'I have listened carefully to all the arguments against accepting the Allied reply now before us. My view has not changed.' The Tenno declared himself convinced of the good intentions of the Allies. He was well aware that even now the nation was prepared to make further sacrifices for its Emperor. 'But I am not concerned what may happen to me. I wish to preserve the life of my people. I will not allow them to be exposed to further destruction.'

Before the Emperor left his audience of twenty-four in a state of profound dejection, he spoke to them like a man who had considered all possibilities and was clear in his own mind:

'As the Japanese people do not know how things really stand, they will, I realize, be deeply shaken when they hear of our decision. If it seems proper that I myself should explain the position, I am ready to go to the microphone. The troops will be particularly shocked by our decision. The War Minister and the Navy Minister will not find it easy to persuade them to accept the decision. I am prepared to go wherever seems necessary in order to justify our conduct. I beg the Cabinet to prepare an imperial edict as soon as possible to announce the end of the war.'

That was the voice of the crane. But the struggle for the armistice was not yet over.

The imperial edict only acquired the force of law when all the Ministers had signed it before the Monarch. If the War Minister refused to sign, he could by his resignation cause a Cabinet crisis and at least achieve a delay.

General Anami summoned the officers of his Ministry to a second meeting. 'The situation is now absolutely clear. Three hours ago the Emperor gave orders that Japan should accept the enemy's terms. The army will obey the Emperor's orders.' As a Japanese, Anami knew—and his friends also knew—that he was responsible to the Emperor for the entire army and that he could not expect to survive the end of the nation's proudest institution. But it was left to him alone to act in accordance with this ancient code of honour, and this gave him the inner freedom to speak to his fellow-officers of the future: 'You officers must understand that even death cannot absolve you from your duty. It is your duty to live and to do your best to help your country find the road to recovery.'

In another, long Cabinet session one Minister after the other, Anami included, signed the document, which sealed the capitulation of Japan. And before midnight Hirohito recorded the proclamation which he had prepared and which was to be broadcast on all stations early the next morning. But the transmission was delayed until midday and frantic efforts were made to supply the electric current for the transmitters, which had been put out of action, while special loudspeakers were installed throughout the country so that the announcement could reach the largest possible audience. The Emperor, anxious to help the broadcasting staff achieve the best results, re-recorded his speech and declared his readiness to record it yet again.

On that sultry summer's night Tokyo, a ghost-city, its ruins in darkness, was the scene of incredible activity. As it seemed too risky to transport the precious recordings of the Emperor's speech to the broadcasting station at night, they were entrusted to two chamberlains, who wrapped them up and placed them in a secret drawer in an ante-chamber occupied by ladies of the imperial court; a pile of books in front of the drawer completed the concealment—a by no means superfluous precaution, as events were to show.

The younger officers were already in a state of revolt, led by Major Hatanaka of the War Ministry and Major Koga, son-in-law of the notorious General Tojo (who was later to be hanged as a war-criminal). The conspirators pinned their hopes on General Mori, who, as commandant of the First Guards' Division stationed in the precincts of the imperial palace, occupied a key position. But the ascetic Mori, who was known as 'the monk', was not prepared to disobey his orders, not even when it was argued that the sovereign had been wrongly advised. His brother-in-law, a Lieutenant-Colonel who had arrived from Hiroshima, was with him when Hatanaka and his fellow-conspirator, Captain Uehara, stormed into the room. The first surviving witness who entered the room after them saw the General and the Lieutenant-Colonel lying in a pool of blood; Mori had been shot, while his brother-in-law's head had been severed from his body by one furious sweep of a sabre. Hatanaka took possession of the commandant's secret seal and used it to issue order after order. The entire palace-grounds were soon in the hands of the rebels. The Director of Information and his colleagues were seized and held prisoner. A feverish search was made for the recordings of the imperial proclamation and the court-officials were subjected to a close cross-examination. All contact between the Emperor's entourage and the outside world was cut. The broadcasting station was occupied and Major Hatanaka took over the studio to broadcast his own early morning news. He did not notice, however, that the operators had taken the precaution of disconnecting the apparatus.

The Emperor, who was a light sleeper, heard the excited whispers of the two chamberlains in the antechamber. When the situation was explained to him, he offered to speak to the mutineers himself.

Quite independently of the palace guard, other units had also spontaneously revolted. The military airfield at Atsugi was in a state of uproar. A group of the dreaded Kemeitai Secret Police attempted to force their way into the house of the Lord Keeper of the Privy Seal but were driven off by the guard. Kido himself lay hidden in a cellar of the imperial palace, waiting for that ghastly night to end.

That same night Captain Sasaki, who was stationed in Yokohama, decided to take steps to save the Fatherland. He mustered a group of 37 soldiers, students and other youths and set off hot-foot for Tokyo. His first objective was to settle accounts with the arch-traitor, Prime Minister Suzuki. His official residence was attacked by machine-gun fire and the building itself set on fire. But Suzuki was in his private house, where he was warned in time and was able to seek refuge with relatives before the Resolute Men arrived, searched every room and finally burnt the house down. They then moved on to the residence of the President of the Privy Council Hiranuma, but this bird too had flown, so that they had to be content once more with setting the house on fire.

While all these dramatic events were taking place, General Anami paid a courtesy visit to the Prime Minister and then returned home. There he chatted with his brother-in-law, Lieutenant-Colonel Takeshita, and together they drank several cups of his best *saké*. The War Minister got ready to take his leave with as much circumspection as if he were going on a pilgrimage. After he had composed his letter of resignation, he took the brush and Indian ink and wrote two final messages in large characters. Then, as dawn began to break, he stepped on to the balcony overlooking the garden and committed *seppuku*. Of the two blood-bespattered sheets of paper he left, one contained his own epitaph:

After tasting the profound benevolence of the Emperor, I have no words to speak.

GENERAL KORECHIKA. *The night of 14 August 1945*

The other message ran:

For my supreme crime I beg forgiveness through the act of death.

And on the reverse side of the paper he had added:

I believe in Japan's sacred indestructibility.

General Tanaka, Commander-in-Chief of the troops stationed in east Japan, had his headquarters in the Daiichi Insurance Building, and his powerful support was sought to prevent the imperial proclamation. But Tanaka was no gambler, and, as soon as the situation at the headquarters of the Guards' Division was explained to him by telephone, he acted with the utmost promptness and vigour. When the car flying his standard drove up to the entrance of the imperial palace and the Commander-in-Chief himself stepped out in front of the stupefied sentries, the whole flimsy structure of mutiny began to tremble and before long Tanaka's air of grim determination brought it crashing down. The three chief conspirators, Major Koga, Major Hatanaka and Lieutenant-Colonel Shiizaki committed *seppuku*, each in his own fashion. Hatanaka left the following epitaph:

I have nothing to regret, now that the dark clouds have disappeared from the reign of the Emperor.

After the Commander-in-Chief had ensured that law and order had been re-established in Tokyo, the two recordings of the imperial proclamation were transferred from their hiding-place to the broadcasting station and the Japanese people were told that a special announcement was to be made.

On the stroke of twelve the usual announcer, whose name was Wada, declared: 'A broadcast of the utmost importance will now follow. All listeners will please stand. His Majesty the Emperor will now read his imperial message to the people of Japan. We respectfully transmit his voice.'

The Japanese national anthem was played and then Hirohito solemnly addressed himself to 'his good and loyal subjects':

'After pondering deeply the general trends of the world and the actual conditions obtaining in Our Empire today, We have decided to effect a settlement of the present situation by resorting to an extraordinary measure. We have ordered Our Government to communicate to the Governments of the United States, Great Britain, China and the Soviet Union that Our Empire accepts the provisions of their Joint Declaration.

'The war situation has developed not necessarily to Japans' advantage, while the general trends of the world have all turned against her interest. Moreover, the enemy has begun to employ a new and most cruel bomb... Should We continue to fight, not only would it result in an ultimate collapse and obliteration of the Japanese nation, but also it would lead to the total extinction of human civilization...

'We are keenly aware of the inmost feelings of all of you, Our subjects. However, it is according to the dictates of time and fate that We have resolved to pave the way for a grand peace for all the generations to come by enduring the unendurable and suffering what is unsufferable...

'Unite your total strength, to be devoted to construction of the future. Cultivate the ways of rectitude, foster nobility of spirit, and work with resolution—so that you may enhance the innate glory of the Imperial State and keep pace with the progress of the world.'

Today if one asks people who heard this speech for their impressions—and almost everyone living in Japan at that time heard the broadcast—it is hard to find anyone who really understood the Emperor's words. The phraseology and the intonation belonged to the world of the court, which was still cocooned in its sacred traditions. But everyone understood the meaning of what was said and realized that this was the end of an era and that Japan had to make a fresh beginning.

With the same determination that marked Japan's adoption of Chinese culture and of the Meiji reforms, she embarked upon this new course, which the American occupation authorities mapped out with their well-meaning missionary zeal.

Under the 1951 Constitution Japan remained an empire. The Tenno is still 'the symbol of the State and the unity of the people', only he no longer derives his authority from his divine descent but 'from the will of the people, in whom sovereignty resides'. Never again can the name of the Tenno be misused, but never again, even in the hour of need, will the voice of the crane be heard.

The wheel of history goes on turning. The enemy of yesterday is the ally of today, fear has turned to admiration, gratitude to a newly resurgent hate, interests and ideologies compete for the control of the economy and of the nation's instincts, and even the most modern clichés which have been adopted from the outside world are somehow not entirely free of the Kami from the 'Land of the Gods'.

THE COUNTRY

With its hundreds of inhabited islands, its thousands of rocky isles and crags, Japan, more than any other country in the world, is an island-empire. The peaks, and ridges, the high valleys and passes tower up like semi-submerged mountain ranges. In none of the four main islands is the centre more than sixty miles from the sea-shore, so that there is no room for any major network of rivers. Four-fifths of the country is very mountainous and consists largely of forest or barren rock. The few 'plains' deserving of the name are confined to the northern half of the country, such as, for example, the Kanto plain around Tokyo which emerged from the sea at the beginning of the Glacial Drift and the Ishikari plain on the island of Hokkaido.

A characteristic feature of the Japanese landscape, particularly in northern Honshu, as well as on Hokkaido and Kyushu, is its many volcanoes. There are about 165, including those in the Kurile and Ryukyu Islands, of which some 45 are active. The frequency of earthquakes is often, though wrongly, ascribed to volcanic action. Such disastrous earthquakes as that of September 1923 in Tokyo were tectonic in origin and there is no historical record of any volcanic eruption, including Fujiyama which has been dormant for two hundred years, affecting an area outside its own immediate vicinity.

The earth's crust is still mobile enough to produce an unusually large number of hot springs, more than a thousand of which are famous for their medicinal properties and have been frequented since time immemorial by all classes of the population.

The Japanese archipelago, which stretches over twenty-seven degrees of latitude and is bounded in the south-east by the Pacific, in the north-west by the seas bordering the continent of Asia, has a rich variety of climates: from the sub-tropical Ryukyu Islands and the southernmost parts of Japan proper to the cold vegetation zones of Hokkaido and the islands to the north of it one finds a highly representative assortment of the world's plants.

Life in Japan, as in the entire eastern and south-eastern fringe of Asia, is largely conditioned by that climatic phenomenon, the monsoon. These peculiar changing winds occur in half-yearly periods as land and sea winds. In eastern Japan the monsoons usually blow from the north-west in winter and from the south-east in summer. Although they are not so violent as the south-westerly summer monsoon in the Indian Ocean, they do make Japan one of the highest rainfall areas in the world.

In spring and particularly in the autumn, between the propitious monsoons, dangerous whirlwinds, the typhoons, occur. They were a major threat to sailing-ships and when the Dutch first started trading with Japan, they reckoned that one out of every three ships would be lost.

Another important feature of the coasts of Japan—they embrace an area of approximately 180,000 square miles and cover a distance of at least 17,000 miles—is the ocean currents. The warm *kuroshio*, coming from the south, washes the coasts of Kyushu, Shikoku and the east of the main island, Honshu, then, farther north, curves towards Alaska. A subsidiary current passes through the Tsushima Strait to the east side of the Japanese archipelago. A counter-current, the cold *ogashio* or Kamchatka Stream, comes down from the north and a parallel current of cold water, the Liman Stream, flows down from the Gulf of Tartary along the Manchurian-Korean coast.

This climate, which shows an over-all rhythmic consistency but is subject to acute localized fluctuations, impinges upon a very varied geological structure. The large number of fairly recent volcanic formations, the steepness and picturesqueness of the mountains, which are mainly composed of gneiss and archaic slate, and finally the strong erosive effect of the mountain streams, all combine to provide the wooded heights and the deep valleys with streams that begin as rushing torrents, become smooth-flowing rivers and eventually form lakes, and there is almost a profusion of rapids, waterfalls and other scenic beauties.

A peculiarity of Japan's mountain formation, which has an important bearing on the position of her towns and communications, is that it consists of two roughly parallel chains, which run the entire length of the country and which slope down towards the Sea of Japan. Lateral ridges projecting from these chains divide the main islands into a large number of valleys or cavities which frequently run right down to the sea. The erosion caused by the humid monsoons helps to provide the river-beds with plenty of gravel which finds its way down to the river-mouths and enables towns to be built where otherwise space would be too limited.

The 'Japanese' people, which today inhabits these islands and has built up Japan's history, bears little resemblance to the original tribes. The Ainu, who are regarded as the 'first settlers', who were pushed back more and more to the north and who are probably of Proto-Nordic origin, play as humble a role today in their few villages on Hokkaido as do the North American Indians in their reservations.

Even before the Meiji Restoration Japan was one of the most densely populated and intensively cultivated countries in the world. On the other hand, only about 15% of the land is cultivable. More than 65% of the landscape has an inclination of 15% or more and 75% of it is covered with forest. In the 13th century the population was about five million, in 1700 about twenty-five million and the first census in 1872 at the

XXII *On the dance-stage of the Itsukushima Shrine on Miyajima (ills. 59, 60) a Bugaku dancer wearing the horrible mask of a Chinese general performs one of the pantomimic dances that go back to the Tang period.*

XXIII *In a procession at the Higashi-Honganji Temple at Kyoto (X, 163) the ancient temple-music is also rendered with pipe and drum.*

XXIV *(Overleaf) Scene from the No play 'Funa-Benkei' (ill. 159): an apparition in a mask threatens Yoshitsune, sitting in the foreground on the left, with a sword; on the right, towards the back of the stage, before the inevitable pine decoration sit two of the four musicians who accompany the play with three drums of varying sizes and a pipe.*

beginning of the Meiji Restoration showed thirty-five million. In 1967 the hundred-million-mark was reached. The rapid increase in population in the 20th century led to a speedy growth in the number of industrial and commercial towns, especially around the two focal points in central Honshu: the Kanto plain with Tokyo in the east and the three cities of Kyoto, Osaka and Kobe in the west. The population density of 694 to the square mile is only exceeded by Holland and Belgium but is in fact much higher if one takes into account the uninhabited mountainous areas. The average size of the land cultivated by a peasant family is less than 2½ acres and more than half the rural population has to have a second source of income.

The heavy rainfall—about twice as much as the European average—particularly favours the cultivation of rice, the most important single foodstuff in east Asia: about 73% of the cultivable land is given over to it. The tea-plant, which was also introduced from China, is particularly widely grown in the Kyoto area and in the Shizuoka prefecture. Mulberry trees for silk production are found mainly in the prefectures of Nagano, Gifu, Yamanashi, Saitama and Fukushima. Intensive vegetable cultivation has been developed particularly around the large cities. About a million Japanese earn their livelihood by fishing, which is still a more important source of food than the livestock industry which has grown up more recently.

XXV *Scene from a Bunraku play in Osaka with the puppet manipulated by three men (see also ill. 162).*

XXVI *Scene from a play in the Kabuki theatre, which shows a typical Japanese living-room with the picture-niche (tokonoma) on the right.*

PREFECTURES

HOKKAIDO:

1 Hokkaido

HONSHU:

2 Aomori
3 Iwate
4 Akita
5 Yamagata
6 Miyagi
7 Fukushima
8 Tochigi
9 Ibaraki
10 Gunma
11 Saitama
12 Tokyo
13 Chiba
14 Kanagawa
15 Shizuoka
16 Yamanashi
17 Nagano
18 Niigata
19 Toyama
20 Ishikawa
21 Fukui
22 Aichi
23 Gifu

24 Mie
25 Wakayama
26 Kyoto
27 Shiga
28 Nara
29 Osaka
30 Hyogo
31 Hiroshima
32 Okayama
33 Tottori
34 Shimane
35 Yamaguchi

SHIKOKU:

36 Kagawa
37 Tokushima
38 Kochi
39 Ehime

KYUSHU:

40 Fukuoka
41 Nagasaki
42 Saga
43 Kumamoto
44 Oita
45 Miyazaki
46 Kagoshima

NOTES ON THE PLATES

1 Fujiyama (Fujisan), 12,395 feet, is the highest peak in the volcanic Fuji chain, which runs diagonally across central Honshu, and is also Japan's highest mountain. For centuries poets and artists have vied with each other in extolling the beauty of this mountain-pyramid, which is a place of pilgrimage visible for a great many miles around and which has become Japan's national emblem. The last major eruption of the volcano, which is now practically extinct, was in 1707.

2 Sulphur fumes rising from the 'Valley of Hell' on Tateyama. The Tateyama massif—the highest peak, Oyama (about 9,700 feet), is one of the 'three sacred mountains of Japan', the others being Fujiyama and Hakusan—forms part of the volcanic Norikura range of the Hida mountains, the 'northern Alps', in the 'Japan Alps National Park' of Honshu.

3 The extinct volcano Zao in the 'Zao Quasi-National Park' in northern Honshu consists of a series of peaks which rise to a height of 5,700 feet and provide ample scope for mountaineering and skiing (ill. 40).

4 Mount Aso in the 'Aso National Park' of Kyushu is a volcanic mountain group rising to over 5,000 feet with five peaks, one of which, the 4,300 feet-high Nakadake, is still active. The largest of its five craters, which is about 2,000 feet across and which can be reached by a funicular (sometimes closed on account of eruptions), constantly belches out smoke and fumes.

5 Air photograph of Fujiyama from the north-west with Lake Motozu, one of the five small lakes north of the mountain.

6 A trip on the Inland Sea (Seto Naikai) between the islands of Honshu, Shikoku and Kyushu provides the traveller with a constantly changing panorama of mountains and mostly wooded islands, peninsulas and bays.

7 Washu-Zan, a hill on the Kojuna peninsula on Honshu, gives a magnificent view of the Inland Sea.

8 The Japanese coasts are rich in picturesque rock-formations. Here we see one in the Otamoi region near Otaru, which forms part of the 'Niseko-Shakotan-Otaru Coast Quasi-National Park' on Hokkaido.

9 The Minogake rocks on the coast of the Izu peninsula.

10 Close to the shore of Futami-ga-ura on the Shima peninsula, which forms part of the 'Ise-Shima National Park', stand the 'Wife and Husband Rocks', Myoto-iwa, on the larger of which stands a *torii*. They represent Izanagi and Izanami, the mythical founders of Japan. At the beginning of each year the straw rope which joins them together is renewed.

11 Fishermen on the beach at Onjuku in the Chiba prefecture.

12 'Ama'-diver on the island of Tsushima in the Nagasaki prefecture searching for the edible sea-snails known as 'awabi'.

13 Fishermen on the beach at Izu, who use their nets also for gathering the seaweed so popular with the Japanese.

14 In a village on the Miura peninsula fishermen are mending one of the nets they use for deep-sea fishing.

15 Lake Shinji, covering an area of 325 square miles, on the Shimane peninsula of Honshu is famous for its abundance of fish, which are being caught here in large landing-nets.

16 In one of the fish-markets, which supply the enormous demand of the large cities. The annual yield of the deep-sea, coastal and sweet-water fisheries is about five million tons.

17 Cultivating the rice-fields on the Kii peninsula.

18 Work in the rice-fields is done largely by women. This photograph was taken near Fukuoka on Kyushu.

19 Rice-fields at harvest-time on one of the few large plains in Honshu.

20 About 73% of the agricultural land is given over to rice-growing. From antiquity, rice has been cultivated in paddy-fields and in feudal times ownership of land was assessed on the basis of the annual rice yield in 'koku' (about five bushels). But rice only became a basic ingredient of the Japanese diet, even among the poorer classes, following the Meiji reforms when its cultivation became intensive.

21 Wakasagi fishing-boats on Lake Kasumiga-ura in the Ibaraki prefecture. Covering an area of some 70 square miles, this is the second largest lake in Japan.

22 Among the most famous of Japan's coastal landscapes is the Bay of Matsushima, the 'pine-clad island', with its hundreds of tiny islets.

23 Peasant girl with her boat on one of the canals, which traverse the rice-fields in the Ibaraki prefecture.

24 In the valley of the River Daiya near Nikko.

25 Magari village near Takayama in the table-land of Hida, Gifu prefecture (see also ills. 113, 117).

26 Landscape in the 'Aso National Park' on Kyushu.

27 Tea-plantation on Honshu. Some 85,000 acres are covered with plantations to provide Japan's national drink. The rows of bushes, about 2½ feet high, either form tea-gardens on the hill-sides or act as hedges in the open fields. Of the annual yield of over 80,000 tons about 10% is for export. More than 90% of the crop is the green tea, so popular with the Japanese, of which there are six varieties, the ordinary *sen-cha* being the most widely used.

28 Tossing green tea in the Shizuoka prefecture, where half Japan's tea is cultivated.

29 Tea-shop display in a suburb of Kyoto.

30 From up on the 3,000 foot-high Koyasan, where Kobo Daishi founded the famous monastery in 816 (colour plates VI, XIX, ill. 72) one looks down on the thickly-wooded slopes of the 'Koya-Ryujin Forest Park'.

31 Myo-o-do in the Mudoji valley is one of the monasteries that were built on the 2,750 foot-high, wooded Hieizan north-east of Kyoto around the original monastery founded in 788 by the first patriarch of the Tendai sect, Dengyo Daishi.

32 The Temple of Muroji in old Yamato, like so many other Japanese shrines, is situated in the middle of a grove of giant Japanese cypresses. More than 60% of Japan's surface area is covered with forest, and timber is the country's traditional building material.

33 Below Lake Chuzenji near Nikko the Kegon waterfall plunges over 300 feet into the gorge beneath.

34 The Katsura, which flows past Arashima east of Kyoto, is one of the many comparatively small rivers of Honshu,

which with their wooded landscape, their gorges and their rapids provide unusually varied attractions for boating parties.

35 In the 'Yoshino-Kumano National Park' on the Kii peninsula lies the Doro-kyo gorge, through which the River Kitayama winds its way: it has the reputation of being the most beautiful of the many navigable gorges on Honshu.

36 The 9,600 foot-high Kai-koma is one of the peaks of the Akaishi range in the 'Southern Alps National Park' on the borders of the Nagano and Yamanashi prefectures.

37 Manza Spa in the 'Joshin-Etsu Highland National Park' at the foot of Mount Shirane is one of many thermal baths in the mountain valleys of Honshu.

38 In the north of the 'Japanese Alps (Chubu-Sangaku) National Parks' is the most northerly peak of the volcanic Norikura range, the 9,500 foot-high Shirouma.

39 The village of Mori in the Nagano prefecture owes its name as the 'village of apricots' to the large number of magnificent apricot trees that grow there.

40 Ski-ing in the 'Zao Quasi-National Park' (ill. 3)

41 On the ski-slopes of Naeba in the 'Joshin-etsu Kogen National Park' on the border of the Nagano and Niigata prefectures. At week-ends and during the winter holidays there is a virtual migration from Tokyo and other large cities by train and bus to mountainous areas in the north, where winter-sports have become extremely popular.

42 It is only since the Meiji reform period that Sapporo, capital of Hokkaido, has developed from a village partly inhabited by Ainus into the largest town north of Tokyo. The streets are laid out on the American checkerboard pattern. The choice of the town as the site for the 1972 Winter Olympiad was dictated by the fact that snow lies here from November until March and the surrounding country provides ideal skiing conditions. The outstanding local event is the Yuki Matsuri Snow Festival, when a competition is held for the building of snow-men and ice-men in in the streets.

43 Towering up in the 'Towa Hachimantai National Park' in northern Honshu is the quiescent volcano Iwate, 6,600 feet high.

44 An Ainu chief in one of the few villages of Hokkaido where this people still survives. The origins of the Ainu, who with their Caucasian racial characteristics are strikingly different from the main Japanese stock which was predominant in historical times and was largely Mongol, are uncertain. At one time they were also present in large numbers on Honshu but today there are only some 17,000 of them left—half their number at the turn of the century—in about a hundred villages.

45 Ainu family in their hut.

46 The laborious work of planting rice-shoots in the marshy Awara district on the north coast of Honshu is done by women, who stand up to it better than men. They walk on wooden blocks submerged in the mud and have straw wrapped round their bodies to keep them warm in the cold water and enable them to 'swim'.

47 In the mountain health-resort of Tanji in the Aomori prefecture members of the same peasant families meet every summer to enjoy the communal hot bath, which is an old Japanese tradition.

48 On the north-west coast of Honshu: an inhabitant of the Tsugaru peninsula in the Aomori prefecture returns home along the Matsumae coastal road with purchases for the New Year Festival.

49 Even in severe winter weather the fishermen of Hokkaido go about their work.

50 An old woman on the island of Hateruna, which belongs to the Yaeyama group of the southern Ryukyu Islands, shows the tattoo-marks (*irezumi*) on her hands which were formerly a common feature.

51 On the Ryukyu Islands it is the duty of the priestesses (*tsukasa*), at periodical ritual festivals to which men are not admitted, to pacify the forces of nature and ensure a good harvest. Here three priestesses are seen at prayer on the coral ledge on the southern shore of the island of Hateruma.

52 Swans in flight over Lake Hyo in the Niigata prefecture.

2

3

4

5

8

9

22

23

27

28

29

43

44

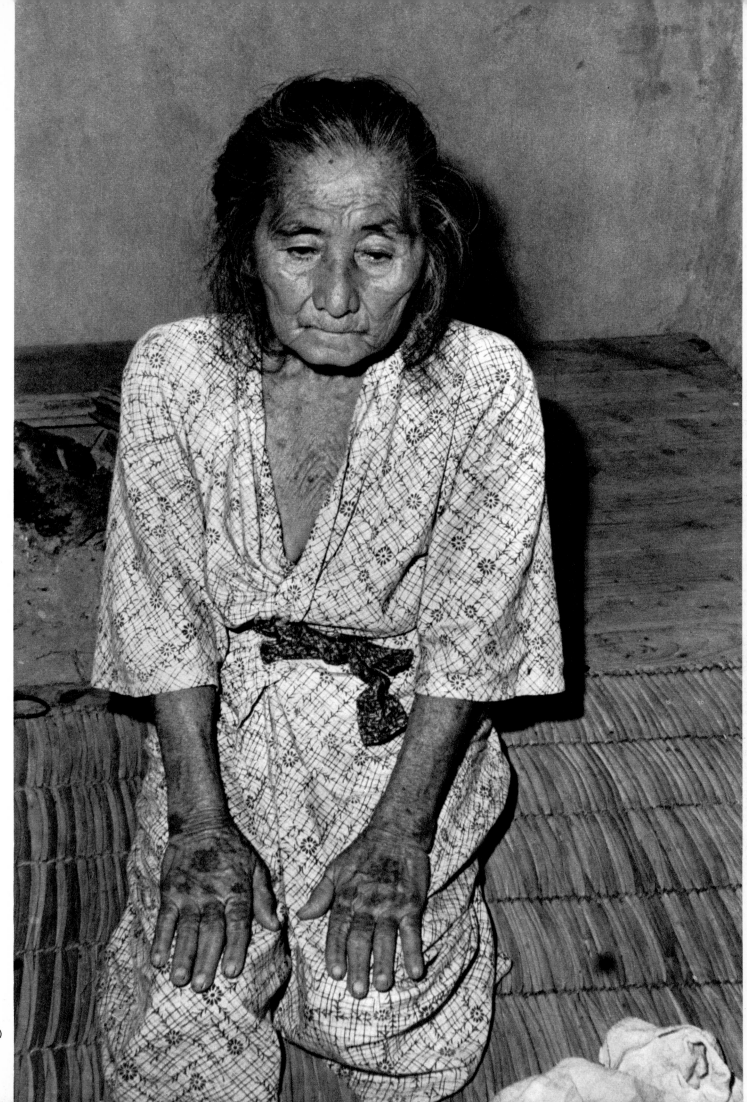

50

BUILDINGS AND GARDENS

Japan's monuments, like her landscape and history, though extremely varied are at the same time remarkable for their uniformity and constancy. Even in the most remote valleys and on lonely mountain-tops one encounters the same *torii* of wood or stone, usually painted red, which marks a shrine of the Shinto or Kami faith, and everywhere one finds the same kind of shrine with the steep, protecting roof and crossed gable-beams. And throughout the centuries Buddhist gateways, temples and multi-storeyed pagodas have retained the same basic Chinese style. The secular palaces and upper-class houses continue to use the same standardized straw mats, the same kind of sliding partitions between rooms surrounded by a gallery, the same kind of gardens, tea-houses, stone-lanterns and fences and the same underlying pattern can be found in the feudal castles, which all date from roughly the same era and which had the same great walls regardless of the region over which the daimyo ruled. Only the houses of the fishermen and peasants developed their own local style.

The traditional building material of Japan is the wood she obtains from her forests. Stone was used only for defence-works and to underpin larger buildings. Innumerable religious and secular buildings were sooner or later destroyed by fire, but most of them were rebuilt quickly and with little change. For example, the main temple of the Shingon sect on Mt Koyasan, the Kongobuji, dates from 1861; the pagoda (*kompon daito*), which forms part of it and was burnt down several times, was last rebuilt in 1937, the Golden Hall (*kondo*), destroyed in 1926, was rebuilt in 1932; the main gateway (*daimon*) dates back to 1705 and only the *fudodo*, built in 1198, has survived in its original form. Restoration in Japan does not mean the conscious preservation of a particular period of architecture, which has been long since superseded, but the perpetuation of a constantly renewed tradition.

The older style of Shinto shrine with its curved, thatched roof, its single-storey timber-work, partly supported by wooden pillars, and the fences and gates surrounding it give one some idea of the architectural style of the pre-Buddhist Yamato, which was characteristic of the earliest palaces. Originally the shrines were only left standing for a short time after they had been built for the annual festival of the deity in question. One of the oldest Shinto buildings, the Naiku shrine of Ise, where the sacred mirror bequeathed to the founder of the imperial dynasty by Amaterasu is preserved, is an instance of a perpetuated tradition which must be unique of its kind in the world: since 685 the buildings with their gilded beam-ends have been demolished every twenty years and rebuilt on the adjacent site with newly-cut Japanese cypress in exactly the same dimensions and proportions as previous generations of carpenters had worked to.

This strict adherence to a style which had become hallowed by time did not prevent the all-pervading influence of China from making itself felt eventually in Shinto architecture and satisfying the growing need for greater display. Thus the Itsukushima shrine with its magnificent gateways, halls and passage-ways reminds one much more of a Buddhist temple than of the original Shinto shrine. And in contrast to the exclusivity and pure style of the national shrine at Ise, the two innermost enclosures of which are only accessible to members of the Imperial family, other shrines such as the Inari-Jingu in Fushimi, a suburb of Kyoto, or the Meiji shrine in Tokyo, are essentially popular meeting-places with, every now and then, a colourful and busy market just outside. As a rule entry to the Kami shrines is by way of several *torii* and past numerous stone lanterns and great, carefully-protected trees.

After the Kami faith of the Shinto a second religious wave broke over the country from China, namely Buddhism; 'shrine' architecture was followed by 'temple' architecture. The great turning-point in Japan's history, personified in the Prince Regent Shotoku Taishi, was reflected in the impressive monastic temples of the 7th and 8th centuries. In Horyuji and the near-by Nara, at the heart of ancient Yamato, the first Buddhist temples appeared, which, with their ornamental sculpture, are among the finest monuments of world art, so nearly unsurpassable that subsequent artists could only strive unceasingly to achieve more delicate and more luxuriant nuances in a changing environment.

The Temple of Horyuji, like most oriental monastic temples or palaces, comprises a whole series of buildings of different kinds and the over-all pattern was adopted in many subsequent building-complexes. Within the confines of the sacred precincts, round the Golden Hall *(kondo)* containing the principal idol are grouped the five-storeyed pagoda *(gujunoto)*, which as the repository of the sacred relics introduces the vertical element in an essentially horizontal scheme; behind is the Hall of Prayer and Sermon *(kodo)*, and beyond that the repository of the Holy Scriptures *(kyozo)* and the bell-tower *(shuro)*. The main entrance is a magnificent two-storeyed gateway.

The Chinese model was also adopted for the construction of a capital city, after the abandonment of the superstition that the residence of the ruler became unclean with the emperor's death and must be moved elsewhere by his successor. Gemmyo Tenno, when he designed Nara in 710, modelled it on Chang-an, seat of the Tang emperor, and the same ground-plan was adopted by Emperor Kammu in 794, when he elevated the place called Udo to the 'Capital of Peace' *(Heian-kyo)* and became the founder of Kyoto. Still a prosperous city, it is surrounded by a vast rectangle of walls on the pattern of the walled Chinese cities and is traversed by wide streets which follow the four points of the compass. In the centre, like a town on its own, is the palace of the Tenno; its row of single-storey buildings are periodically reconstructed in the same perishable wood.

The early Buddhist buildings such as the Golden Hall of Horyuji with the majestic Sakya Trinity, or the Todaiji Hall in Nara with its great wooden pillars supporting the roof over the fifty-foot-high bronze statue of the Buddha, show a predilection for sheer size to which Japanese architects and sculptors were less and less prone as they broke away from the Chinese influence. Axial effects and symmetry which tend to produce grandeur are contrary to the Japanese feeling for nature. For while continental China with its vast spaces showed an awareness of the free movement of wind and water in the Feng Shui but never lost sight of the cosmic harmony and saw evidence of a higher dispensation at work even on earth, for example in pointing the sacred mountains towards the four corners of heaven, the island-empire followed the eternally varied and asymmetrical lines of its own landscape. And so in building the most formal of tombs, the vastly expensive shrine in honour of Tokugawa Ieyasu in Nikko, the Japanese no longer modelled themselves on the Chinese imperial tombs with their long passages and monumental flights of steps leading up the mountainside; the steps leading to the entrance-*torii* are hidden under great trees and from there turn sideways to the ceremonial door in front of the main halls and turn yet again before reaching the tomb itself, so that at no point does one have a clear view of the whole site.

In the course of the centuries the basic design of shrine, temple and dwelling-house took on a great many different forms. There were periods when a purely Japanese style was predominant, others when new ideas were imported from the Sino-Korean mainland, and while the tendency at court was towards greater splendour, an underlying strain of ascetic simplicity kept breaking through. The monasteries with their growing wealth vied with the court and feudal nobility in building temples, private dwellings, gardens and pavilions of great artistic distinction. Through the open galleries nature penetrated the interior from the gardens, and the artists who decorated the niches and screens also took their themes from nature. The pervasive influence of the Ch'an-tsung school of meditation with its admixture of Taoism found its most concrete expression through the Zen sects in what is perhaps the purest and noblest form of Japanese self-realization, the tea-ceremony, which, whether in a monastery, in an imperial country palace or in a private house, always has something of the casual informality of a modest peasant cottage: with impeccable taste the simple timber architecture, the vessel for the water, the stone-flagged path and the mossy garden are all perfectly blended.

A special feature of Japan's architecture is the great daimyo castles which were built in the last quarter of the restless 17th century, before Ieyasu stopped the feudal barons constructing their fortresses. With their massive stone walls, their deep moats and the keep high up in the centre, accessible only through several rings of fortifications, they could hardly be bettered as defensive buildings, and no photograph can adequately convey their size and overpowering strength.

Paul Claudel said that European culture reflected nature, while Japanese culture imitated it; the one seeks to express itself, the other to express nature. The European builds 'without sympathy for the earth, solely concerned to achieve the widest possible field of vision', while the Oriental shuns broad landscapes and hankers after 'that communion of viewer and view, for which all that is needed is to linger'. And so the garden is as much a part of the living-room in a private house as in a monastic community; it becomes the most subtle expression of a culture which seeks harmony with nature, keeping the wilderness at bay with tireless green fingers, a work of art which, without our expert care, degenerates into chaos. Mountain and stream, the towering pine and the tender green carpet of moss, the rush of the waterfall, the mirror of the lake and the endless expanse of the ocean, all this is contained within the small but constantly changing world of the garden. In the rock-garden of the Zen monastery the eye is caught by the deeply-furrowed sea of sand, from which a rocky island, sparsely ringed with moss, emerges, and one is reminded of the 'innate sense' to which the priest Dogen, founder of the Soto school, dedicated the lines:

> In spring cherry-blossom,
> In summer the cuckoo,
> In autumn the moon,
> And in winter snow, pure and cold.

53 The simplest and oldest form of Shinto shrine is to be found in the buildings at Ise, which are set in a grove of cedar-trees: simple wooden houses with poles supporting the roof of crossed beams, the joints of which have neither nails nor dowel-pins and demand highly skilled carpenters. The timber used is from specially selected Japanese cypress trunks (Cryptomeria; in Japanese, *hiroki*).

54 The naiku or inner shrine is the focal point of the Jingu shrines of Ise and of the Shinto cult in general; here the sacred mirror Yata-no-Kagami, associated with the goddess Amaterasu, ancestress of the Japanese nation, is preserved. In the foreground the empty space which alternates with the present site every twenty years (1953, 1973, etc.) when the buildings are renewed. The main shrine (*shoden*) is surrounded by a fourfold palisade; the two innermost precincts may only be entered by members of the imperial family.

55 The Izumo Taisha Shrine, also called Oyashiro, in the Shimane prefecture, is regarded as the oldest shrine in Japan. It is said to go back to the legendary palace of the Okuninushi-no-Mikoto, God of Healing and of Agriculture. The main shrine, which is surrounded by a double wooden fence, was last renewed in 1744. Together with the 'shimmeizukuri' of the Ise shrine, it represents with 'taishazukuri' the other oldest variant of the original Shinto buildings, which presumably also approximate to the style of the pre-Chinese palaces.

56 The small shrine on the way up to the volcano Aso may serve as an example of the buildings which were erected in endless varieties and sizes, but always on the same basic pattern, throughout the length and breadth of the land in honour of the local deities (*kamis*).

57 The Kumano Nachi Shrine of the Kii peninsula is said to date from the 4th century.

58 *Torii* to the Toshogu Shrine in Nikko (see also ill. 105–107). The *torii*, a gateway of wood or stone, usually painted red, is the emblem of the Shinto or Kami creed; countless examples of these, generally attached to a shrine, are to be found all over Japan.

59 The Itsukushima Shrine on the island of Miyajima in the Bay of Hiroshima is dedicated to the three daughters of the god Susano-o-no-Mikoto. Standing on wooden posts, founded in 811 and renewed at regular intervals, this building with its halls connected by galleries shows the influence of Buddhist temple architecture. The landmark of this place, which ranks as one of the three 'classical landscapes' of Japan (*nihon san kei*), is the great red *torii*, which towers out of the water during the flood season.

60 Among the buildings which form part of the Shrine of Miyajima, next to the open stage for the Bugaku and Kagura performances (colour plate XXII) is reputedly the oldest No stage still extant. The roof is covered with cypress bark. On the left, the passage (*hashigakari*) through which the musicians and actors enter the stage. The theatre dates from 1568 and was renewed in the Edo period.

61 The Temple of Horyuji near Nara was built by the Prince Regent Shotoku Taishi in 607 and subsequently extended. The main buildings are not only the oldest Buddhist structures of their kind in Japan, they are also believed to be the oldest surviving wooden buildings of their size in the world. Rare in themselves, they also contain works of art which go back to their foundation and which, like the architecture, have a marked Chinese flavour. In this air view one can distinguish in the inner precinct before the Great South Gate (*nandaimon*) the two-storey Middle Gate (*chumon*) on the left, the Golden Hall (*kondo*, ill. 62) in the centre on the right, the five-storey pagoda (ill. 64) to the left of it, the Hall of Sermon (*daikodo*) behind, the Sutra Library (*kyoro*) in the two corners on the left, and the bell-tower (*shuro*) on the right. On the right, outside the covered passage, is the long Hall of the Holy Spirit (*shoryoin*), beside it the narrow building in which the sacred vessels are kept (*kofuzo*).

62 The Golden Hall (*kondo*) of Horyuji is 30 ft long, 24 ft wide and 58 ft high. Splendid cantilever beams support the deeply-projecting, tiled, double roof. The temple, founded in 607, was burnt down in 642 and a few years later rebuilt in a slightly changed form.

63 The Sermon Hall (*daikodo* or *kodo*) of the oryuji Temple with its characteristic coffer ceiling contains the Yakushi Trinity in gilded wood, in which Buddha is worshipped as the healer, surrounded by celestial guards.

64 The five-storey pagoda *(goyu-no-to)* of the Horyuji Temple, a masterpiece of timber construction, is built round the great hundred-foot-high central pillar, which rises up into the nine-ringed corona. The beams, which date from 607, were dismantled during the war and, when the danger had passed, were reassembled.

65 The main idol of the Horyuji Temple in the Golden Hall is the three-foot-high image of Sakyamuni, the historical Buddha, which was cast in bronze in 623 and which is flanked on either side by the Bosatsus Yakuo and Yakujo.

66 The treasure-house Shoso-in in the temple precincts of the Todaiji at Nara is a rare example of a storehouse built on wooden piles (*azekura*); its walls consist of triangular beams, the ends of which project outwards. The Shoso-in houses the 8th-century masterpieces of pottery and metalwork deriving mainly from the collection of the Emperor Shomu.

67 In the Hokkeji Temple of Nara, a convent founded by the Empress Komyo in the middle of the 8th century, stands the three-foot-high sandalwood image of the eleven-headed Juichinen-kannon (Avalokiteshvara), which dates from the 9th century.

68 The focal point of the 'Great Eastern Temple' (Todaiji) of Nara, headquarters of the Kegon sect, is the Hall of the Great Buddha (Daibutsu). The huge fifty-foot-high figure represents the original Buddha Birushana-Butsu (Buddha Vairocana) making the gesture (*mudra*) of teaching (*seppo-no-in*). The original design is attributed to a Korean, Kurinaka-no-Kimimaro. The statue, cast eight times, was completed in 749 after years of preparation and in 752 was consecrated in the presence of the imperial court and of 10,000 priests. The head was broken-off during an earthquake in 855 and a fire in 1180 caused the head and the right hand to melt. In 1567 the head was again destroyed by fire but was once more restored in the original style.

69 To the right of the Daibutsu in the Todaiji is an image of the Nyoirin-Kannon in gilded wood from the Genroku period (1688–1704).

70 In the *mieido*, founder's hall of the Toshodaiji Temple at Nara, the wooden figure of the blinded Chinese priest Ganjin (Chinese: Chien-chen), founder of the temple and of the Ritsu sect, is preserved. It is said to date from 763, the year of his death.

71 The Daibutsu Hall of the Todaiji Temple at Nara (see also ills. 68 and 69) was built in 745–752 and burnt down in 1180. It was promptly re-consecrated in 1195 in the presence of Emperor Go-toba and Shogun Yoritomo Minamoto. In the civil war of 1567 it was again burnt down. The present building dates from 1709.

72 The buildings of the great temple on Koyasan, the centre of the Shingon sect (colour plate VI) founded in 816 by Kobo-Daishi, were frequently ravaged by fire, and only the *fudodo*, the Hall of the Fudo, has remained intact since 1198.

73 The Daibutsu or Great Buddha of the Kotokuin Temple at Kamakura, which belongs to the Jodo sect, was originally, like the even bigger Daibutsu of the Todaiji at Nara, roofed over but after the hall was destroyed by a spring flood in 1495, it was not restored. The 37ft-high bronze statue, originally a Shaka, later reinterpreted as Amida, was cast in 1252–55 to the design of an unknown artist.

74 On the bronze lantern which stands before the Daibutsu of Kamakura is carved, amongst other things, a relief showing Kannon holding a stool shaped like a lotus-flower, which represents a seat in Amida's paradise.

75 Nishi-Honganji, the parent monastery of the Jodo-Shinshu sect founded by Shinran, with its complex of buildings, its gardens and its works of art is one of the finest temples in Kyoto. From the *daishido*, founder's hall (on the right

in the picture), a covered passage leads to the *hondo*, main hall, with the sacred image of the Amida-Nyorai. The hall was rebuilt after a fire destroyed it in 1760.

76 The two-storey gateway San-Mon of the Kenchoji Temple at Kamakura was rebuilt 1755. The temple is the headquarters of a branch of the Rinzai school of Zen Buddhism. The Hojo regent Tokiyori founded it in the 13th century to accommodate the Chinese priest Tai Chiao (Daigaku-Zenji), who had come to Japan after the fall of the Sung dynasty.

77 The pagoda of the Hompoji at Kyoto, by contrast with the more frequent five-storey pagodas, is in the Tahoto style, in which a flat, white-plastered hemisphere serves as the link between the square substructure and the upper storey, reminding us that the pagoda was a development of the Indian stupa. The temple belongs to the Nichiren movement and was founded by Nisshin in 1436.

78 On the north side of the Engakuji, one of the Great Zen temples of Kamakura, stands the 'House of the Yellow Plums', Kobai-in, a plain building, which the famous priest and poet Soseki (1271–1346)—posthumous name: Muso-Kokushi—is said to have constructed.

79 On the coast of the Miura peninsula stands a tea-house, which belongs to the imperial summer villa of Isshi and which has a thatched roof that is reminiscent of similar roofs from very ancient times.

80 Ginkakuji, the 'Silver Temple' at Kyoto, was originally built by the Ashikaga Shogun Yoshimasa, a connoisseur of the arts, as a country seat after his abdication and was later converted into a temple-monastery of the Rinzai school. The 'Silver Pavilion' of 1483, the main building in the magnificent gardens, is one of the chief monuments of the Muromachi period. The original plan to cover the roof with silver never materialized.

81 Among the most popular examples of Buddhist imagery are the stone figures of Jizo at the roadside—in this case near the Chuzenji Temple—representing the *bosatsu* who is the patron-saint of travellers, pregnant women and children.

82 The Temple of Muroji goes back to the early period of Buddhism in Japan: it was rebuilt by Kobo-Daishi in 824. The five-storey pagoda, although much repaired, is one of the rare original monuments left from the early Heian period.

83 The East Room (*higashi-no-ma*) of the abbot's apartments (*hojo*) in the Zen temple of Daitokuji at Kyoto gives an impression of the decorous splendour of a sophisticated interior during the Momoyama period. The sliding-doors are decorated with paintings of the Kano school, the floors covered with bamboo mats. The temple was already famous for its treasures in the Middle Ages but had to be restored following fires in 1453 and 1468.

84 The rectangular rock garden of the Nanzenji Temple at Kyoto, belonging to the Rinzai school of the Zen sect, contains like the famous rock garden of the Ryoanji the 'abstract' reproduction in sand of a wind-furrowed sea from which isolated islands of rock emerge and which is intended to encourage contemplation.

85 Zen monk contemplating the rock garden of Daisen-in, one of the lesser temples in the temple-enclosure of Daitokuji at Kyoto. The design of the garden, in which the stones emerging from the sea of sand are, in part, reminiscent of the towering rocks in a picture of the Chinese school, is attributed to the 77th abbot of the monastery, Shuko Kogaku (1465–1548).

86 Water container for the tea-ceremony at the pool in the temple-garden of Chishakuin at Kyoto, headquarters of the Chizan branch of the Shingon sect. The design of the garden is ascribed to the master of tea-ceremonies Sen-no-Rikyu (1522–91).

87 A Geisha in the garden of the tea-house scoops clear water from the fountain with the specially-prescribed tea-ladle for the tea-ceremony.

88 Water-container in the tea-room garden of the Zuiho-in, one of the 22 temples in the grounds of the Daitokuji at Kyoto. Zuiho-in was founded in 1546 by Sorin Otomo, who was then a Zen monk but later became daimyo on Kyushu and one of the champions of Christianity.

89 On the occasion of a flower-show in the Sorakuin Garden at Kobe a competition is held for masters of *bonsei*, the art of miniature-gardening with dwarf trees in a shallow bowl, which has been practised since the Heian period.

90 Part of the garden of Daisen-in (ill. 85) south of the abbot's apartments, which represents the ocean in pure white sand. The monks (sometimes attired in Western clothes) who tend the garden must regularly rake the sand and build it up into heaps.

91 Stone lantern in the garden of the Zuisenji Temple at Kamakura. The *kasuga* type is one of the most popular of the many different styles of lanterns in shrines and temples as well as in private gardens.

92 The Shoi-ken tea-house, built in the unadorned style of a peasant's house, in the imperial garden of Katsura near Tokyo.

93 The Ritsurin Park at Takamatsu, where the Matsudaira clan formerly had their country seat, covers 180 acres and is one of the most extensive and most famous landscape-gardens on Shikoku.

94 The Kenrokuen Park at Kanazawa (Ishikawa prefecture) was designed in 1819 by the daimyo Narihito Maeda. It shares with the Kairakuen at Mito and the Korakuen at Okayama the reputation of being one of the finest landscape-gardens in Japan.

95 One of the corner-towers of the vast compound, surrounded by walls and moat, in the centre of Tokyo, which was the official residence of the Tokugawa shoguns in the Edo period and which has been the Imperial Palace since the Meiji reform period.

96 Air photograph of the Imperial Palace at Kyoto. The site of the palace built by the Emperor Kammu in 794 was moved after a fire in 1788 to the centre of the town, where the buildings had to be restored after yet another fire in 1854. But the original design with its formal symmetry after the Chinese style was retained.

97 The castle of Kumamoto was built 1601–07 by Kiyomasa Kato, daimyo of the Higo province. The impressive fortifications withstood a fifty-day-long siege in 1877 by a rebel army equipped with fire-arms, until relief came. The keep in the centre, surrounded by steep battlements, was rebuilt in reinforced concrete in 1960 and made into a museum.

98 The castle of Osaka was built 1584–86 of massive granite blocks by Hideyoshi Toyotomi as the seat of his power. In 1615 the fortress was destroyed by Ieyasu's troops but was later rebuilt by the Tokugawa. In 1868 it was set on fire by supporters of the defeated Shogunate, but was reconstructed once again in reinforced concrete in 1931, when the 135 foot-high central tower was erected.

99 Hirosaki in the Aomori prefecture was the seat of the Tsugaru clan, who built their castle here with the characteristic multi-storey keep.

100 Nagoya grew up round the castle of the Imagawa (subsequently of the Oda) clan and became one of the first towns (today the third largest) in the country, after Ieyasu Tokugawa had built a new castle for his son Yoshinao in 1612. This enormous building was bombed during the war and restored in 1959 to serve as a museum.

101 Odawara, one of the main stages on the Tokaido Road running from Edo to Kyoto, was the fortified seat of the Hojo clan (not to be confused with the Hojo of the Kamakura period), which dominated the Kanto Plain in the 16th century. The four-storey castle tower was restored in 1960.

102 The castle of Himeji, round which a flourishing industrial town grew up on the road running westwards from Kobe, is regarded as the finest of the impressive castles of the Momoyama period. The building goes back to a fortress

erected by Sadanori Akamatsu in the 14th century, was enlarged in 1581 by Hideyoshi, further extended by his General Terumasa Ikada in 1600 and took final shape in 1615–24.

103 Before modern industrial techniques were introduced into their country, the Japanese had developed bridge-building to a high degree in order to carry the roads across the many rivers. One of the most famous bridges of the Edo period is the Kintai Bridge, also known as Soroban-bashi (abacus bridge), spanning the River Nishiki. It was built in 1673 by the local daimyo, Hiroyoshi Kikkawa. About 600 feet long, it has no nails and its five arches rise to 40 feet above the water; it was swept away by flood-water in 1950 but rebuilt in 1953 to the original design.

104 The Sanjo Bridge (sanjo means 'third road') over the River Kamo on the outskirts of Kyoto was built by Hideyoshi in 1590. A milestone on the bridge designates it as the first station on the Tokaido Road.

105– The third Tokugawa shogun Iemitsu built the Toshogu Shrine at Nikko as a mausoleum for Ieyasu, who had been
107 given the title of 'Incarnation of the Bodhisattva illuminating the East'. The buildings, which were constructed under the supervision of Kora Munchiro by the finest workmen from Nara and Kyoto, combine motifs from Shinto shrines and from Buddhist temples. The golden and richly-coloured ornaments are for the most part the work of the wood-carver Hidari Jingoro. The almost overpowering splendour of the building is tempered by the exquisite refinement of detail and the background of hillside covered in tall trees produces an over-all picture of solemn grandeur.

Ascending the Sennin Ishidan steps ('thousand-people stone steps') one reaches the granite *torii* (ill. 58), which bears the name of the shrine inscribed in the handwriting of the Emperor Go-Mizuno-o. Particularly beautiful is the gate leading into the central court, the Yomei-mon (Gate of Sunlight, 107), in whose niches two of the most powerful predecessors of the first Tokugawa shogun, Yoritomo and Hideyoshi, (colour plate XII) stand guard. Very nearly as impressive is the Karamon (Chinese Gate, 105), decorated with dragons, behind which lies the Hall of Offerings (*haiden*). Among the wood-carvings on the walls are the three monkeys (106), also popular in Japan, which by their gestures illustrate the wisdom of the saying: 'See nothing, hear nothing, say nothing.'

108 The town of Kurashiki is noteworthy for its unusual civil architecture which contrasts with the traditional wooden buildings; with its massive walls and its stone bridges spanning the canal that runs through the old town, it reminds one of Chinese towns.

109 Entrance to a private house in Kyoto, which, as is customary in the older quarters, has only one storey and is secluded from the outside world by means of a gateway.

110 A special feature of Kurashiki (ill. 108) is the storehouses for the rice grown in the surrounding Okayama Plain. The Archaeological Museum, which was opened in 1950, was built in the style of these storehouses.

111 Living-room of the superintendent of a fishing combine of the Izu peninsula; in the foreground of this typical rural interior is the hollow in the ground for cooking, in the background on the right the dining-table, in the left background the small house-altar.

112 A peasant house in the Shizuoka prefecture; it has a typical thatched roof and a rectangular garden in front.

113 This particularly splendid example of a peasant house from the Hida province (see also ill. 25), where pointed gables are a feature, has the rare distinction in Japan of having several storeys.

114 Fishing village on the island of Sado (Niigata prefecture), its roofs, like those of Alpine huts, weighted down with stones.

115 The village of Ishigaki-shi on the island of Ishigaki, part of the Yaeyama group belonging to the southern Ryuku Islands. In this region the traditional method of house construction takes into account the perils attendant upon frequent tornadoes: the sturdy houses are surrounded by protective walls of coral-stone and their roofs of pampas grass are reinforced.

116 Peasant house on the outskirts of Kyoto.

117 The living-room in one of the imposing houses in Hida (see also ills. 25, 113).

53

55

73

74

The Japanese possess to a unique degree the ability to combine receptiveness to everything new with loyalty to traditional custom. Tradition for them is not the antithesis of progress, a reactionary clinging to all that is old. Even when they are in rebellion, they are still motivated by romantic memories of the civil wars and the raids of medieval knights.

Anyone who has seen a Japanese theatrical, film or television production may have noticed how the measured movements, the very epitome of self-discipline, suddenly give way to an outburst of unbridled passion. The climax is reached when the display of towering rage or agonizing pain achieves its artistic fulfilment in the particular medium employed. One may be reminded of the art of a Corneille, but Corneille is essentially a man of his time; he represents one of those Western epochs whose mode of expression already seemed out of date to the next generation.

Reports by the very first European travellers show that they were particularly impressed by the Japanese form of suicide, this ultimate test of knightly valour. In the medieval battles of the Taira and Minamoto the defeated general killed himself in a away that developed into the ritual suicide known as *seppuku*. Although in 1663 the Edo Shogunate forbade the samurai to commit suicide, *seppuku* was still served as an honourable death-sentence until the early years of the Meiji Restoration, and in very recent times still it was regarded as the supreme token of loyalty to the Tenno: General Nogi, for example, the victor of Port Arthur, killed himself together with his wife, when the Emperor Meiji's funeral cortège left the palace, and in August 1945 General Anami, the last imperial War Minister, chose the same method of accepting responsibility for the capitulation. Dignity and a sense of beauty are qualities that must also go with a peaceful departure from life, and famous priests, statesmen and generals, to say nothing of ordinary mortals, have expressed their last thoughts in short poems; thus the poet-monk Ryokan (1758–1831) took leave of the world with the words:

> What shall be my legacy?
> The blossoms of spring,
> The cuckoo in the hills,
> The leaves of autumn.

The desire to achieve control of the body through the mind has resulted in a way of life that seeks to reconcile rigorous self-discipline with grace and sensibility, and so that strange combination of ethical and aesthetic precepts has emerged, which motivates so much of everyday life in modern Japan: in the much-admired meditations of the Zen monks but also in social life, in the manner of greeting someone, of drinking tea, of decorating one's house, of cultivating one's garden, and finally in an all-embracing courtesy, the formalism of which would almost seem to be rooted in the ritual of a bygone age of the gods.

In the traditional arts and crafts the master still relies partly on instructions passed down from generation to generation. In the No Theatre, for example, the rules laid down by Se-ami around the year 1400 are still followed and direct descendants of the original No masters are still to be found in the No companies. The kimono, which is still universally worn at least as a house-coat, was originally a costume of the Tang period in China. In the objects with which the Japanese surrounds himself, from the simple rice-bowl to the precious ritual object, one is always conscious of a strong sense of form and an instinct for simple beauty.

During the period of the Kamakura Shogunate, under the influence of Zen Buddhism, the culture of the warrior-monk developed, and in the Muromachi and Momoyama periods the court nobility and the leading monasteries brought the art of living to its most advanced form, stimulating the writing of poetry, for example, by means of competitions, establishing the tea-ceremony and the art of the *ikebana*.

This is not the place to enlarge on the theme of language and poetry, which forms such an integral part of Japanese culture, but one example may suffice to show how even such powerful war-lords as the three Unifiers of Japan expressed themselves on the same theme in three *haiku*, the short poems consisting of 5 + 7 + 5 syllables, which are ascribed to them. The first of the Unifiers, Oda Nobunaga, wrote the following:

> If he will not sing,
> I shall slay him,
> The cuckoo.

He was succeeded by the boisterous Toyotomi Hideyoshi, who dearly loved luxury:

> If he will not sing,
> I regard him silently,
> The cuckoo.

It was left to the last of the Unifiers, Tokugawa Ieyasu, to write:

> If he will not sing,
> Then I wait until he sings,
> The cuckoo.

The tea-ceremony *(chanoyu)*, which was devised in the Zen monasteries of Kyoto, became the most refined expression of the Japanese way of life. It is designed to bring man, outwardly and inwardly purified, into harmony with the universe and, by quiet participation in Life, to give him an awareness of his true self. Paul Claudel wrote of the tea-ceremony as it is practised today in many more or less traditional forms: 'Nothing is simpler, it would seem, than to prepare tea, to light the fire, to pour in the water; to infuse the precious leaf, to breathe in that odorous vapour which is spirit rather than beverage, the vegetable soul of this burning earth. But each of the successive acts has been determined by an elegant and inflexible ritual, to which the executor adds only an imponderable element of grace and of dignity, veiled by the prescribed gestures. For here one learns from infancy that in all things, even if they be evil, there is a good and a bad way of behaving.'

Ikebana, the art of arranging flowers and branches, has also retained something of the simple solemnity of a cult, and the aesthetic rules of the various *ikebana* schools reflect in many different ways the magical relationship between heaven, man and earth.

The Tokugawa period saw no striking new social or cultural developments though the most was made of the rich heritage of previous epochs, but what had been largely a privilege of the upper class and the rich monasteries became more and more widespread. The tea-ceremony was no longer confined to temple gardens and princely courts but became an essential part of every young lady's education. *Ikebana* was preached in every cultured household, and knightly sports became increasingly popular. The art of printing, introduced from China in the Nara period, took a great leap forward with the acquisition of type-printing from Korea, which Ieyasu encouraged and which led to an unprecedented distribution of classical literature, while the great masters of the woodcut were able to satisfy the demand of a growing number of art-collectors.

The culture of the Tokugawa period, which spread to the middle-class, made its outstanding contribution in the world of the theatre. While the No-theatre was particularly active at the shogun court of Edo, the dancer Okuni, who first appeared at the shrine of Ise, created in the Kabuki what is still the most popular dramatic form. Song and dance combine with play-acting and, by contrast with the strict formalism of No, all the technical potentialities of the stage—including a new invention, the revolving stage—were exploited in order to present the romantic war-epics and love-stories in as realistic and colourful a form as possible. At the same time, thanks to the Japanese code of honour and courtesy, even the Kabuki performances developed that highly stylized art, which the woodcuts of Utamaro, Sharaku and others so fascinatingly interpret.

The various popular forms of puppet-show also gave rise to an extremely effective dramatic art, after the Joruri singer Takemoto Gidayu and the puppeteer Yoshida Bunzaburo had joined forces and found an outstanding author in the dramatist Chikamatsu Monzaemon. The Bunraku puppet-show, named after the man who revived it in 1811, at one time displaced even the Kabuki in popularity.

Dances and music such as are still performed today range from the ancient pantomimes of the shrines and temples to the revues, which have also become historical, of the two Geisha theatres in Kyoto, from the archaic Bugaku of the imperial court to the countless festivals in the provinces, where all kinds of picturesque customs have been preserved connected with the worship of local gods.

The Japanese are an extraordinarily festival-minded people. In addition to the annual festivals which are celebrated throughout the country, such as Children's Day or more precisely Festival of Boys, *Kodomo-no-hi*, and the Dolls' or Girls' Day, *Hina Matsuri*, which falls in the peach-blossom season, individual shrines, temples and towns celebrate their own commemoration days with splendidly colourful decorations, processions, dances, fireworks and performances of all kinds, in which the young people can kick over the traces of normal, day-to-day life. One could fill volumes with representations of these customs and we must confine ourselves here to a few isolated examples.

NOTES ON THE PLATES

118 A Japanese artist in his home: Shinsui Ito (b. 1898) carries on the tradition of *ukiyoe* painting which flourished in the Edo period. His studio at Zushi near Kamakura is furnished with the usual *tatami* mats and on the small tables are the brushes and the porcelain dishes containing the various colours. The sliding doors—those inside with the traditional paper covering, those outside with large panes of glass as the sole concession to modernity—open on to the gallery which surrounds the house and to the garden with its small tea-house.

119 Traditional handicraft: in one of the small silk factories of Kyoto coloured prints are transferred to one of the long strips of silk for a kimono.

120 The doll-painter Takezo Takahashi in Narugo (Miyagi prefecture) painting his *kokeshi*, the cylindrical wooden dolls which are traditional to this district of north-eastern Honshu (ill. 169).

121 The master-potter Isso Yagi in his workshop at Kyoto. Despite the advent of mass-production, pottery is still

practised and cherished as a form of art based on a long tradition, which has also influenced modern arts and crafts in the West and which is constantly producing new and highly imaginative works.

122 In the Nishijin quarter of Kyoto silk-brocades, which have been famous for centuries, are still produced on hand-looms, crowded together in a dark room.

123 An *ikebana* master teaching a class in Tokyo. *Ikebana* or *kado*, the art of arranging flowers and branches, was developed under the Ashikaga shoguns and became universally recognized as an essential ingredient of the sophisticated way of life in the Edo period. A variety of styles along more formal or more natural lines have evolved, all of which observe their own, carefully devised, inherent laws of nature.

124 Girls playing the *koto*, a traditional Japanese musical instrument.

125 In the geisha schools of Kyoto the young girls, who are to help entertain the guests in the tea-houses, are instructed in all the rules of sophisticated living, principally singing, playing the *samisen*, dancing and the art of the tea-ceremony.

126, The tea-ceremony (*chan-no-yu*), demonstrated here by geishas, has become a symbol of social culture and its
127 ritual origins are still recognizable. The choice of locality, the utensils used and every single action are all governed by precise rules but the actual performance also calls for great personal charm. The climax comes when the guest is offered a cup (*chawan*) of tea, after the green powder has been taken from the tea-caddy (*chaire*), hot water has been poured on it and stirred with a bamboo-brush (*chasen*).

Tea came to Japan as part of the cultural invasion from southern China and its enjoyment, more particularly by the Zen monks, was developed into a ritual, in which Taoist customs played a part and whose observance bore some resemblance to that of the Lord's Supper. Then the great tea-masters of the 15th and 16th centuries created the tea-ceremony as such, which in its many variations, from simple serving by the host to the strict observance of a ceremonial lasting some three hours, survived an early setback during the Meiji reform period.

128 Shichi-go-san, i.e. Seven-five-three, is the feast that falls on 15 November, when children of these ages, namely seven-year old girls, five-year old boys and three-year-olds of both sexes, are dressed up in ceremonial clothes and taken to the shrine of their local patron deity or to another shrine—in this case the great Meiji Shrine at Tokyo. The custom dates back to the imperial court in the Heian period.

129 On Sundays young people practise *go-ju-ryu*, a form of karate, in the grounds of the Peace Centre at Hiroshima.

130 Judo—'the gentle path'. Holding down your opponent from the side, known as *joku-shiko-gabarro*.

131– Sumo wrestling is the most popular public display of traditional sport. As long ago as the Heian period 'giants'
133 engaged in contests at the imperial court and the rules which still apply today were evolved during the *sengoku*, the civil wars in the 15th and 16th centuries. Each year three of the great national tournaments for professional wrestlers weighing from 90 to 150 kg. (198 to 330 lb.) are held with all the traditional ceremonial in the Kokugikan Hall in Tokyo.

134 Kendo, the kenjutsu of the samurai in the Edo period and already practised as *tachiuchi* in the Nara period, is the typical Japanese style of fencing. In modern kendo the duellist often uses a bamboo-stave instead of a sword and is protected by a bamboo-shield, padding over his loins, thick gloves and a fencer's mask. During the period of militarism kendo was compulsory at schools but was forbidden after 1945 by the occupation power; it was re-admitted in 1951 and has again become extremely popular, as seen here in the fencing hall of Waseda University in Tokyo.

135 Harunori Otsuka, karate-master of the Meiji University, giving instruction.

136 Kendo-fencers (ill. 134).

137 Archery, originally practised by hunters and fishermen, then principally by warriors, has remained to this day one

of the most popular sports, surviving even the introduction of fire-arms; daily practice in the art serves to keep the Imperial Palace Guard in Tokyo physically fit and mentally alert.

138 At the annual festival of the Tsurugaoka Hachimangu Shrine at Kamakura the knightly art of the Yabusame is sometimes performed on 16th September, when an archer dressed in the hunting costume of the Kamakura period has to hit three targets from a galloping horse.

139–142 In the *naiku* (inner sanctum) of the Shinto Shrine of Ise (ill 54, 55) on the occasion of an important festival the priests open the chests, which have been carried from one of the treasure-houses (139). Before entering the holy places the visitors cleanse hands and mouth in the crystal-clear water of the River Isuzu (140). The chief priest leaves the small shrine adjoining the *naiku*, the Ara-matsuri-no-miya, where the sun-goddess Amaterasu in her terrifying mani-festation is worshipped (141). In the reception-building of the shrine certificates are displayed to the visitors (142).

143 During the festivities at the great Shinto shrines the crowds jostle in much the same way as at an annual market. Here we see the Tori-no-Ichi, the 'Festival of Cocks', celebrated each November at the popular Asuka shrine in Tokyo, at which the 'kumade', small decorated sticks, are sold as symbols of good fortune.

144 With formal dignity the white-clad priests of the Itsukushima Shrine of Miyajima (colour plate XXII, ills. 60, 61) make daily sacrifice at midday to the three female deities of the shrine. Before the Hall of Purification (*hariden*) one looks into the Hall of Worship (*haiden*) and the Hall of Offering (*heiden*).

145 At the Inari Shrine in the Fushimi suburb of Kyoto, which was founded in 1371 and where the rice deity, Uga-no-Mitama, is worshipped, two Shinto assistant-priests (*sho-gu-ji*) bring an offering which must include raw, washed rice, salt, water and rice-wine.

146 *Omiya maira* ('paying homage to shrine'): the presentation of a child-in-arms at the Minatogawa Shrine, also known as the Nanko Shrine, in Kobe.

147 On the occasion of the 'small' or peasants' New Year festival, i.e. on the day of the first full moon in the New Year, the inhabitants of Nishiyokoyama (Niigata prefecture) assemble in the village shrine, where the Shinto priest per-forms the Toshikoi ritual to ensure a good harvest in the new year. The peasants have already cleansed themselves by bathing in the cold water of the River Kuwatori.

148 A country Shinto procession with a portable shrine in the Fukushima prefecture illustrates the simplest and oldest form of these ceremonial processions, which become particularly splendid occasions in the big centres.

149 During the Harvest Festival, which lasts for several days in June, at the village shrine of Ohama on Ishikagi, one of the southern Ryukyu Islands, the arrival of the Miruku (Miroku-bodhisattva) is celebrated as a 'god of visitors' coming from beyond the sea. The belief in numinous powers from the sea and beyond the sea, which work for good or evil, plays a major part in the folk-religion of these islands.

150 On the stage of the Inari Shrine in Kyoto (colour plate VII, ill. 145), which was built as a No stage, Kagura dances are performed daily by girls belonging to the shrine. The girls, dressed in red and white and popularly known as *miko-san*, do duty in the shrine for a certain time and also carry out all kinds of practical work. Their official designa-tion is *kami* (deity)—*hoshi* (service)—*suru* (make)—*joshi* (virgin).

151 The musicians at a Shinto shrine with their ancient pipes.

152 As in the Miyajima Shrine (colour plate XXII), performances of the Kagura dance with demon-masks are also held in the Shrine of Ise. This ritual dance, Kami-no-kura, which dates back to the earliest period of Japanese civilization, means literally 'Seat of the Deity'.

153 Pupils in a Zen monastery at Kyoto engaged in *zazen*, sitting in meditation in the Hall of Meditation.

154 A Zen professor empties his cup at the tea-ceremony in the tea-house of the Reiun Temple in Kyoto.

155 Pupils of a Zen monastery in their sleeping-quarters with the 'futon'.

156 Monk in meditation in the Zuigan-ji monastery-temple of Matsushima, which belongs to the Rinzai school of Zen Buddism.

157 Scene in a No play (see the No theatre in Miyajima, ill. 60): left, the covered gangway (*hashigakari*) across which the actors pass from the mirror-room (*kagamino-ma*) and slowly enter the stage, on the rear wall of which there is always a picture of an old pine-tree (*kagami-ita*). Before the main actors appear, the singers take up their positions on the right, the instrumentalists against the rear wall.

158 Scene from a Kyogen play, a short farce which is inserted between the serious No plays.

159 Scene from the No play 'Funa-Benkei' (colour plate XXIV), which is based on historical events: the victorious General Yoshitsane (front left), who is pursued by the jealousy of his brother Yoritomo, the first Kamakura shogun, draws his sword against the spirit (with mask) of a Taira warrior drowned in the naval battle of Dan-no-ura, who is threatening him. The actor playing the part of the spirit, Kanze Shizuo, is a direct descendant of the two founders of the No play, Kan-ami and Ze-ami.

160 Cherry-blossom dance in the Gion Kaburenjo, one of the two geisha theatres of Kyoto, where the performances are concentrated in a spring and an autumn season. The geisha dance Miyako-odori was introduced in 1872 by Inone Yachiyo, the third dancing mistress (*iemoto*) of the same name.

161 Scene from a performance at the Kabuki theatre in Tokyo. Kabuki, since the Edo period the most popular form of Japanese drama, employs, by contrast with the austere style of the No, all the arts of stage technique. Wild fighting scenes and attacks—here we see a house with a spirit appearing on the burning roof—alternate with tender confessions of love-pangs and tragic suicides.

162 Of the various forms of Japanese puppet-theatre performed by local troupes the Bunraku in Osaka (colour plate XXV) has achieved a high artistic standard. It originated towards the end of the 16th century from a combination of the puppet-show known as Ningyo and a form of story-telling accompanied by the *samisen*, which is called Joruri after the princess in a romantic love-story. Extremely popular in the 17th and 18th centuries, it suffered a temporary decline, until Uemura Bunraku founded his successful Bunrakuken troupe in Osaka in 1811. While the reciter, who sits on a small side-stage on the right, tells the story with great feeling, accompanied by a *samisen*, the action is mimed on the main stage, each of the puppets, about three feet tall, and its mechanism being operated as a rule by three puppet-players, who all, except for the main actors, wear black masks.

163 Dance by boys representing buds of paradise (*kanyobin*) at a temple festival on the dance-stage of the Higashi Hongan-ji in Kyoto.

164 The troupe of the Imperial Household in a Gagaku performance. Gagaku is the oldest and most distinguished form of Japanese music, which came from China in the early days and was particularly popular at court in the Heian period. It is usually played as an accompaniment to the solemn old Bukaku dances and the music department of the imperial court is making special efforts to preserve it.

165 In the Shinto festival processions—this one is at Nikko—the youthful bearers vie with one another to carry the sacred shrine (*mikoshi*) in order to ensure good fortune for themselves until the next year's festival.

166 The flying of bamboo kites is an extremely popular pastime with Japanese boys, particularly around New Year; at other times of the year, too, various towns—Nagasaki in the spring—hold their own kite-flying festivals. At the Tako-age Festival in June at Shirone (Niigata prefecture) two parties flying kites measuring 25 by 20 feet try to cut the opponent's kite-string.

167 In the shrine at Shiogama, the port of Sendai in the Miyagi prefecture, the patron deities of seafarers and expectant mothers are worshipped. On 9–11 July the shrine celebrates its festival with a procession of picturesque dragon-boats.

168 The main festival at Nagasaki is the Okunchi of the Suwa Shrine held on 7–9 October. The climax of the three-day festivities in the town, which is gaily decorated for the occasion, is the dragon-dance, which recalls similar customs in China.

169 Each year, on the first Saturday and Sunday in October, the town of Narugo celebrates the Kokeshi Matsuri Festival, when these life-size dolls parade through the streets. Other features of the festival are the *kokeshi* contest and a memorial service held by *kokeshi* craftsmen.

170 Tokushima, seat of the prefecture of the same name, celebrates each year on 15–18 August its dance-festival Awa Odori.

171 Tanaba Matsuri, the Festival of Stars, is usually celebrated throughout Japan on the night of 7 July. The legend, which originated in China, relates that once a year two widely-separated stars on the Milky Way, Kengyu (Altair, star of the cowherds) and Shohuju (Vega, star of the weavers), are united. In 755 the reigning Empress Koken is said to have first decreed that this happy event should be celebrated. On this occasion, it is the custom for young people in particular, including schoolchildren, to hang up strips of paper with their offerings and wishes. In Sendai the festival is celebrated with particular pomp on 6–8 August: the houses are decorated with brightly-coloured strips of paper and in the main streets the crowd jostles its way through a forest of glittering decorations.

172 In a Shinto shrine on the Izu peninsula a peasant woman undergoes the exorcization ceremony conducted by a priest wearing a lion-mask.

173 Kennembutsu group in Aomori: during the coldest ('kan') time of the year a group of Nichiren adherents, mostly elderly people, make a pilgrimage from house to house reciting the Buddha-calling formula (*nembutsu*): Nammye-horenge-kyo.

174 At Yohote (Akita prefecture) in northern Honshu on 15 February the children celebrate the snow-festival by building snow-huts called 'kamakura', in which they erect small altars and settle down round the lit candles.

175 On the occasion of the New Year Festival at Nishiyokoyama (ill. 147) the children bring straw and other material to form a pyre, at which the villagers take leave of their patron deity Sai-no-kami, who has been amongst them during the festival.

119

120

131

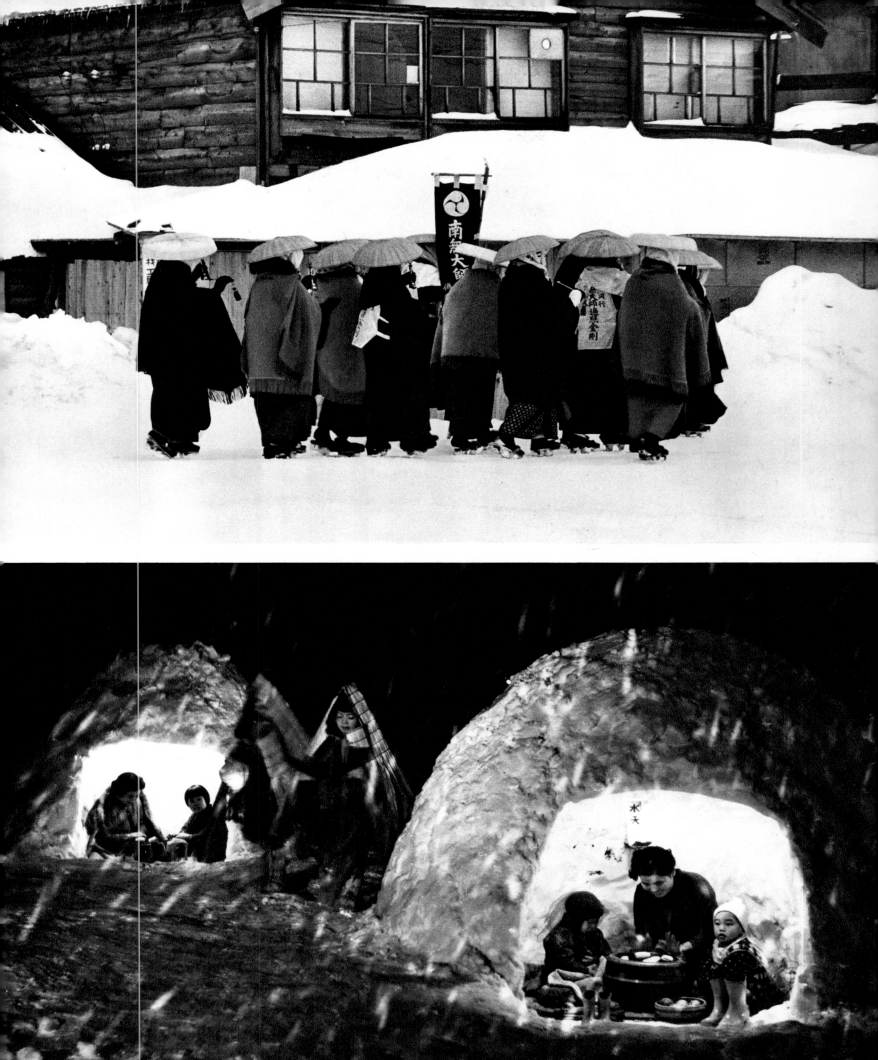

Although the visitor to Japan very soon becomes aware that this is a country rich in tradition, his first impression on landing at Tokyo airport is of a forward-looking people, who are in the forefront of the world's industrial nations and who are therefore exceptional among the countries outside the European-American cultural community.

When Japan, during the Meiji era of reform, advanced straight into the age of technology and global commerce, she brought with her a complete national structure such as no other developing country possessed: these were a central authority which had evolved over centuries and a social system based on kinship; agriculture and the fishing industry exploited to the full the national wealth of a densely-populated country, the artisans had retained all the skills acquired during the periods of great cultural prosperity, and the general standard of education was unusually high.

Anxious to learn from Western civilization, the Japanese looked first to Britain, the pioneer among the industrial and colonial powers. But they also brought in French and German instructors, and the Dutch, who had enjoyed something of a monopoly, lost considerable ground. It was only gradually that the United States, whose Admiral Perry had thrust open the door to the secluded island-empire, became, in the guise of 'neighbours' from the other side of the Pacific, the major contracting party in Japan's economic, geopolitical and military expansion. But the oldest, nearest and biggest partner, China, seemed to be at the mercy of the rival colonial empires around her.

The modernization introduced during the Meiji era embraced all branches of public life, from the Constitution to communications, from education to new forms of industry. Enterprising sons of the impoverished samurai went into commerce, and the family concerns known as the *zaibatsu* emerged, of which the fourteen most powerful controlled almost a third of Japan's entire industry before the war.

The opening of the Tokyo-Yokohama railway in 1872 by the Emperor Meiji—on 14 October by the old calendar, according to the new calendar on 12 September, a day which, since the 1922 Jubilee, has been celebrated as 'Railway Day'—marked the beginning of a rapid expansion of the railway network, in which private lines competed with the State Railways. By 1926 locomotives and other rolling-stock were being manufactured in Japan. Since then Japan's railways have been a model of efficiency and punctuality and the fastest train in the world runs between Tokyo and Osaka, along the old Tokaido road.

New schools for engineers were followed by similar training-colleges for architects; here too the first models were British and palatial banks were liberally supplied with Grecian pillars. The town-centres took on a new, Western look, whereas the residential suburbs still consisted largely of low wooden houses. A fresh impetus came from the Viennese Secession and from America. In 1922 Frank Lloyd Wright was commissioned to rebuild the Imperial Hotel in Tokyo—it has since been replaced by yet another, very much higher and more profitable building. The rapid growth of the cities (in 1965 there were as many as 131 cities with more than 100,000 inhabitants, seven of them exceeding the million mark) and above all the destruction of Tokyo on two occasions—in the earthquake of 1923 and subsequently in air raids—confronted the Japanese architects with tremendous new problems, and the acute shortage of space forced them to build higher and higher. A Japanese school of architects emerged which played an increasingly prominent part in the international style of architecture that has developed in the second half of the twentieth century, and while the influence of Western architects such as Le Corbusier, Gropius and Mies van der Rohe is indisputable, it is also true to say that certain features of Japanese architecture have been adopted in the West, through Bruno Taut amongst others, and more particularly in domestic architecture. So greatly has the Japanese influence affected European and American garden-design that it is almost taken for granted.

In building-up their national industry, the Japanese concentrated, to begin with, on textiles, and by 1933 they had become the world's main exporters of cotton goods. Since then Japan has also gone over to synthetic fibres. As she annexed more and more sources of raw materials and markets, her armaments industry grew correspondingly and, while the first round of hostilities against China and Russia was fought largely with British weapons, from the Manchurian Incident until the catastrophe of 1945 the armaments industry was developed with fanatical zeal to a point where it came to dominate the whole of Japan's national life.

When the Americans landed and, to the astonishment of a population that had been steeped in war-propaganda, behaved not like enemies thirsting for revenge but like missionaries intent upon spreading their ideas of democracy and commerce, the course of Japanese national policy underwent a change almost as radical as in the Meiji era. Korea, Formosa and whatever else had been conquered in the course of previous decades were all evacuated and Japan's 'living-space' was once more confined to the old Shogun empire. The all-powerful military clique disappeared even more quickly than the warrior-caste of the samurai before them and left even less trace of their going; a liberal-democratic constitution was drawn up with a government which was dependent on Parliament but possessed considerable powers, while the Emperor became the 'symbol of the nation and of the unity of the people' and his name could no longer be misused as that of an ostensibly absolute ruler. The powerful *zaibutsu* combines were dismantled—on American orders,—land reform was introduced which broke up the largest estates and turned leaseholders into free peasants, and the educational system was modernized.

The cities were in ruins, the national economy had been crippled by the war-effort, and the people were on the verge of starvation. There were no more foreign mineral resources to feed the country's industry and there was no more foreign manpower. A new social consciousness had been awakened, which demanded that industrial workers should play a new part in the life of society, so that, as time passed, the ability of Japanese industry to undercut world prices by paying starvation wages would gradually disappear, and, if the Japanese were to compete in world markets, they would have to be more scupulous in their use of patents and licences than they had been in the past.

But Japan still had one asset of enormous value: the deep sense of national pride which was shared by all classes of the population and which had survived the shattered dreams of world domination. Despite the fact that a new power had emerged in the trade unions, there were still big industrial concerns, which, with employees and workers engaged for life, were almost patriarchal societies, and soon giant combines appeared again—some bearing the same names as the old *zaibutsu* enterprises—which dominated about half the market, while the other half was supplied, as before, by the countless traditional small firms. Thanks to the shrewd planning of the government, to the ambitious entrepreneurs, and to a highly ingenious system of credit, which channelled all available resources into the rapid construction of new plants, and thanks, not least, to the initial aid given by the occupying powers, a national economy was created which developed at a phenomenal rate and soon made Japan one of the world's leading industrial nations. One must, of course, not overlook the fact that, following her radical conversion from a military to an industrial power, Japan was only spending 0.8% of her national income on defence in 1968 and that expenditure on social services was far below the average for a modern welfare state. This spectacular development occurred while Japan was leaning heavily on one of the super-powers. What sort of course will the Japanese ship of state follow when it is politically free? And what effect will international trading interests, ideologies, social unrest and technology have when the island-empire is drawn once again into the world vortex?

The reconstruction programme which started in 1945 covered the country's entire economic life, even such traditional industries as fishing and agriculture adopting the new methods and machines. The fishing industry, which underwent intense development, has succeeded not only in meeting the large internal demand but also in exporting enough to pay for about a fifth of the imports of foodstuffs. Fish-breeders make use of artificial spawning methods and the sea-weed which plays such an important part in Japanese menus is grown on plantations. The cultivation of fruit and vegetables is on the increase, partly at the expense of the mulberry trees for what has become a less important silk industry. Arable land, which has hitherto been neglected, is being brought under cultivation and the manufacture of synthetic fertilizers is contributing to the increase in productivity. In common with other parts of the world, Japan is modernizing her agriculture at a time when her farming population is on the decline. Between 1868 and 1940 the proportion of the population engaged in farming dropped from 81% to 41%, and it is estimated that by 1985 it will have fallen to 10%.

Some idea of the technological revolution in Japan can be gained from the increase in the use of electric power: whereas in 1935 a mere 24.7 million kilowatts were being used, in 1965 the figure had risen to 192 million. Part of the supply is provided by power stations which have been built in the mountains. Of the various industries which grew up in the Meiji period, shipbuilding has made the most spectacular advance and now has orders from all over the world, particularly for giant oil-tankers, which has enabled the Japanese to take the lead from the British shipbuilding yards and leave them far behind. Typical modern industries such as the chemical and electrical industries, including the rapid growth in computer production, have also advanced dramatically. The highly developed film industry supplies more than 4,000 cinemas (in 1960 there were as many as 7,457!) as well as producing high-quality films for export, but it is being more and more overshadowed by television, which has an audience exceeding twenty million (1968) with the most modern, locally produced sets. The remarkable aptitude of the Japanese worker, both male and female, for precision-work has been reflected in the growth of the watch industry, and the experience they have gained as a people of dedicated photographers has stood the Japanese in good stead in developing the production of cameras. (The photographs reproduced in this book were taken largely by Japanese cameras.)

For a long time it was said of Japanese industry that it depended on the inventions of other nations. Since the 1950's great efforts have been made to improve this image and there is no shortage of salutary self-criticism in the press. Precious foreign exchange is still being spent on acquiring licences from abroad but a great deal more is now being invested in research.

The Japanese were fairly slow to recognize the importance of the automobile. Even after the war long-distance travel was almost entirely by rail and the condition of the roads was far behind that in other industrial countries. The output of motor-vehicles, despite determined efforts to achieve self-sufficiency, remained correspondingly low. But in the sixties, not least because of the Olympiad of 1964, there was a radical change: in 1958 some 200,000 motor-vehicles were produced, by 1966 the number had risen to 2.3 million, and the four million automobiles manufactured in 1968 topped even the West German figure and brought Japanese cars on to the world market. As the industry developed under private enterprise, the network of public highways was extended by the State. Almost overnight four- to six-lane motorways were built on high concrete pillars right through the congested heart of Tokyo, and in 1967 work was started on the construction of 32 highways with a total length of 4,800 miles linking the country's main cities.

Anyone visiting Japan today cannot fail to notice the rapid expansion of the tourist industry. The number of Western-style hotels, some of them masterpieces of modern architecture, increases from year to year, although there is still a preponderance of Japanese tourists. All kinds of facilities, including the usually indispensable interpreter, are provided for the foreign sight-seer, but for the Japanese, however alive they may be to the international customs of the twentieth century, tourism is not a foreign innovation. Its roots go deeper in Japan than in any other country; it is one of those traditions which, although it has adapted itself to modern conditions, remains as popular as ever. One of the earliest masterpieces of Japanese literature is the *Tosa Nikki* of 935 by Ki-no-Tsuryauki, and tells of a journey from the province of Tosa on Shikoku to Kyoto. Visits to the old imperial city with all its monastery-temples, its tea-houses and theatres, pilgrimages to one or other of the famous Shinto shrines scattered throughout the country or to the Buddhist temples, taking the waters in one of the spas tucked away in some peaceful valley or even simple excursions to some spot where the cherry-blossom is at its most luxuriant in spring or where the autumn colours of the sycamores are at their most flamboyant, where the moon's reflection is at its brightest or where the familiar silhouette of Fujiyama can be seen to best advantage—all these stimulated travel and the development of hostelries and transport, particularly after the Tokugawa introduced stability and security throughout the land. Today the most avid sight-seers in Japan are the Japanese themselves. In addition to the countless groups of tourists which are disgorged from the enormous coaches at the Golden Temple of Kyoto, the Ieyasu Mausoleum in Nikko or at the ferry to the Miyajima Shrine, there is also a steady stream of uniformed schoolchildren, eager to learn more about their native land with its fascinating, constantly-changing landscape and its rich cultural heritage.

NOTES ON THE PLATES

176 For the 1964 Olympiad in Tokyo Japan's leading architect, Kenzo Tange (b. 1913), designed the two National Gymnasium buildings for swimming and basket-ball contests. The canvas roofs, a daring innovation, are suspended from steel cables.

177 Hakodate, the second-largest town of Hokkaido with more than 250,000 inhabitants, was one of the first five ports in Japan to be opened to foreign ships under the treaties of 1859, although it had served them as a coaling station since 1855. A funicular railway runs today from the town, formerly the seat of the Kono clan, to Mount Hakodate, which dominates the bay.

178 Nagasaki, capital of the prefecture of the same name and the third largest town of Kyushu with over 400,000 inhabitants, became Japan's main port for trade with the West after the arrival of the Portuguese and Dutch in 1571 and even during the Tokugawa period of seclusion it remained the gateway through which European influence penetrated into Japan. The industrial quarter Urakami was the target of the second American atom bomb on 9 August 1945. Glover Mansion (with a splendid view of the harbour), a typical English residence of the late 19th century, is believed to have served as a model for the setting of Puccini's opera *Madame Butterfly*.

179 The Kyoto International Conference Hall was built in 1966, to the designs of Sachio Otani.

180 The International Hotel of Kurashiki, designed by Shintoro Urabi, is an excellent example of the many 'Western style' hotels, which were built in the 'sixties'.

181 The Sports Stadium at Saga, capital of the prefecture of the same name on Kyushu, was built in 1963 by Junzo Sakkakura (b. 1904), a pupil of Le Corbusier.

182 Exhibition of products of the electrical engineering industry in Hall 2 of the International Trade Centre at Tokyo, which was built by Masachika Murata (b. 1903) in collaboration with the engineer Yoshikatsu.

183 The Sports Stadium of the Kagawa prefecture at Takamatsu was built in 1964 by Kenzo Tange.

184 The Ginza quarter of Tokyo with its large stores, commercial buildings, hotels and places of entertainment is the focal point round which the life of the capital revolves.

185 The number of road vehicles increased by leaps and bounds in the 'sixties and as a result road-building, which had been somewhat neglected in Japan, rapidly developed. In addition to national motor-ways, clearways appeared in the bigger cities, stimulated in the case of Tokyo by the Olympiad, which cut their way through the sea of houses at a higher level than the normal traffic: here we see Clearway no. 4 in Tokyo, opened to traffic in August 1964, at the Akasakamitsuke intersection.

186 In Tokyo and other cities the automatic red telephones, which have been installed at the kerbside, are in constant use.

187 Although the Japanese have produced the most modern portable cameras, the large standard camera from the Meiji period is still widely used for group-photographs. Here it is being employed in the particularly popular setting of the Seiho Pool of the Heian Shrine at Kyoto to photograph a wedding-group, the bride in traditional costume, the ladies, including two nuns with shaven heads, in kimonos, the bridegroom and most of the other men of some standing in cut-aways.

188 Prominent among Japan's sight-seers—shown here in the famous rock gardens of the Ryoanji Temple at Kyoto—are the groups of uniformed school-children and keen amateur photographers.

189 Divine Service in the temple of the Tenri-kyo sect in Tenri.

190 Japanese department stores, backed by years of tradition, offer the highest international quality of consumer goods; the customer is served by white-gloved hostesses, charming exponents of traditional Japanese courtesy.

191 Since the 'fifties, 'Pachinko', a pin-ball game, has become increasingly popular as an innocent pastime in numerous amusement-arcades in Japanese cities—in this case in Kyoto.

192 The square in front of Shinjuku Station in what is after Ginza the main business centre of Tokyo was built 1960–66 on three levels in order to solve the massive commuter problem—estimated at over 1.3 million people a day—created

by the incoming trains and the 68 bus services which converge here. The facilities provided, most of them under-ground, include a shopping centre and parking for 420 cars.

193 An underground station in Tokyo.

194 Street in Ponto-cho, the entertainment quarter of Kyoto, which with its countless attractions has always been the main draw of Japan's internal tourist trade.

195 Japan's mountainous terrain provides ample opportunity for producing hydro-electric power. The largest dam built so far is the Sakuma Dam, completed in 1956, which turns the River Tenryu into a lake in the heart of a remote, wooded part of the country and supplies a power-station with a capacity of 350,000 kw.

196 For many years the Japanese railways have ranked among the most modern and most comfortable in the world. In 1964 Tokyo airport was linked with the city-centre by means of a monorail service, which passes under the runways then emerges to travel over a series of bridges along the Bay of Tokyo to reach the city.

197 On Kojima Bay in the Okayama prefecture a dyke was built in 1956, which reclaimed a large area of new land for cultivation. The dam, which is over 4,000 feet long, also made it possible to shorten communications between Okayama and Uno and to create a sweet-water lake for irrigation.

198 The winter-cultivation of strawberries by the 'Ishigaki method' of planting in concrete blocks on sunny hillsides is one of many examples of intensified horticulture, the products of which are also exported.

199 Sea-weed plantation on Haman Lagoon in the Shizuoka prefecture.

200 Air photograph of one of the large shipbuilding-yards: Ishikawa-jim Harima Heavy Industries Co. Ltd.

201 Shipbuilding-yards at Kobe. This city with more than a million inhabitants lies on the Bay of Osaka and is the main port for the vast agglomeration of industry and commerce of which the cities of Osaka, Amagasaki, Nishinomiya and Ashiya also form part. Nearly 34 per cent of Japan's exports are shipped from here.

202 In the port of Yokohama, the gateway to Tokyo, women are employed as dock-labourers to unload grain. Japan is dependent on imports both in the form of raw materials for her industry and to feed her hundred-million population.

203 In one of the shipyards, where the world's largest tankers are built today.

204 A female precision-worker in one of the world-famous firms producing photographic equipment. The Japanese are extremely keen photographers, and it is by no mere accident that, once that they had ceased to reproduce foreign models, they were able, particularly in this field, to manufacture goods of the highest quality.

205 Engineer in one of the major electrical engineering firms (Hitachi, Tokyo) conducting experiments in a sound-proof chamber. Japanese industry, while continuing to acquire foreign patents, is concentrating more and more on research.

206 Steel-worker at the N.K.K. Works (Nihon Kokan Kawasaki), one of the heavy industrial firms which have to import much of their raw material and which have revolutionized their production methods since the war.

207 Togo Murano (b. 1891), one of the pioneers of modern architecture in Japan, adopted the style of the Momoyama period (1573–1615) in designing the Kabuki Theatre in Osaka, built in 1958 of reinforced concrete with the roof covered in copper plates.

208 The bamboo-shrubs in the courtyard of the Yamato Bunkakan Museum at Nara, built in 1960 by Isoya Yoshida (b. 1894), lend a happy touch of the traditional to a modern functional building.

209 Totsuka Country Club in the Kanagawa prefecture, one of the places that cater for the many lovers of golf, which for decades has been the favourite sport of the upper ten thousand but since the 'fifties with their improved standard of living has attracted more and more people.

210 One of the finest golf-courses is at the health-resort Sengokuhara in the Hakona region at the foot of Fujisan.

211 Students in the university quarter of Waseda in Tokyo—for once not demonstrating (see ill 217, 220) but filled with a desire to learn, which is much more typical of the vast majority of young Japanese.

212 The main building of Hosei University in Tokyo, built 1958 by Hiroshi Oe (b. 1913) who is Professor there. Japan possesses (1966) 346 institutions of higher education, of which 74 rank as national, 37 as public and 235 as private universities.

213 In Tokyo's Ueno Park a Cultural Centre was set up after the war, which includes, *inter alia*, the National Museum for Western Art, designed by Le Corbusier and containing the Matsukata Collection, and the Cultural House built in 1961 by Kumio Mayokawa. In the courtyard an original bronze cast of 'The Burghers of Calais' by Rodin.

214 In Tokyo's stores are held exhibitions, at which leading artists show their works and can always be assured of arousing wide-spread interest. Here is a Paul Klee exhibition hung in the Seibu department store.

215 Japan is today one of the world's leading film-producing countries. Particularly popular are samurai films with their display of chivalry and daring: the actor Toshiro Mifune is here seen playing the part of the Sanjuro Tsubaki in a film directed by Akira Kurosawa (Toho Studio, Tokyo).

216 Rehearsing a characteristic raiding scene from feudal Japan in the film *Eleven Bandits*, directed by Hiroshi Inagaki.

217 The spirit of the Ronin, the bellicose, independent samurai of yore, finds expression not only in Kabuki plays and film scenes but also on the streets in clashes between groups of students on the warpath and the police, who are noted for their toughness.

218 Niju-bashi, the double bridge at the entrance to the Imperial Palace in Tokyo, is the first target for school-children and Japanese tourists visiting the capital. One group after the other climbs out of the buses that pull up in the broad square for the traditional photograph.

219 May Day demonstration in Tokyo. Even the noisy, left-wing agitators have barely shaken the close, almost intimate relationship between worker and employer.

220 Violent demonstrations by predominantly Left-wing groups of organized students have been almost daily occurrences since the 'fifties. Although it is only in their opposition to the existing order in University and State, as well as to the Americans that they are united, many of them, who were the hotheads of yesterday, after passing their examinations become pillars of the 'Establishment'.

221 The Taisekiji Temple on the southern slopes of Fusijan is headquarters of the Soka-gakkai movement, based on the teachings of the prophet Nichiren, which is the most politically influential of Japan's modern religious communities. The number of families belonging to it was 164,000 in 1954; by 1959 it had risen to 1,050,000, by 1969 to 7,218,000. The Grand Reception Hall of the Taisekiji was designed by the architect Kimio Yohoyama.

222 On 10 June 1962 on the Nishizaka Hill at Nagasaki a memorial to the Christians crucified here on 5 February 1597 was consecrated. The designer was Kenji Imagi. The life-size bronze statues of the 26 martyrs are the work of the sculptor Yasutake Funakoshi.

223 The Roman Catholic Cathedral of the Virgin Mary in Tokyo is one of the outstanding works of Kenzo Tange. The 125 foot-high building with its four steep, smooth steel roofs forming a cross holds 2,900 people and was consecrated in February 1965.

224– Hiroshima was a flourishing industrial city of some 350,000 inhabitants, when, at 8.15 on the morning of 6 August
227 1945, the first atom-bomb of the war exploded over the centre of the town, levelling to the ground everything within a radius of two miles and killing some 200,000 people. A law was passed in 1949 providing for its reconstruction as 'Hiroshima Peace Commemoration City', and by 1960 the number of inhabitants was greater than before the catastrophe. On an island between two arms of the river the 'Peace Memorial Park' was laid out and the 'Bridge of Peace' leading to it (224) was designed by Isamu Noguchi. Through the concrete arch of the cenotaph designed by Kenzo Tange for the victims of the atom bomb (225) one can see the steel skeleton of the dome of an exhibition hall, the sole remaining relic of old Hiroshima. In front of the Peace Memorial Museum is set up a free-standing group by the sculptor Arata Hongo (227), showing a mother fleeing with her child. In the grounds between the cenotaph and the ruin a perpetual flame burns (226).

228 A modern country school. Japan's school system is based on an edict of 1872 by the Meiji government, which was radically modernized in 1947 and which has given Japan a lower rate of illiteracy than even some cultivated nations in the West can boast. After the war the construction of new schools became imperative not merely because many buildings had been destroyed but also because the growth of the population and the raising of the compulsory school-attendance period from 6 to 9 years had brought an increased demand. Instead of the old wooden buildings there is a preference for pre-fabricated houses and reinforced concrete constructions, which stand up better to the frequent earthquakes and typhoons. Responsibility for elementary schools rests with the village and municipal authorities.

229 With a healthy, happy youth Japan hopes to overcome the problems of the future.

186

187

188

195

196
197

211

213

Chronological Table

Glossary of Japanese Terms

Index

Photographic Sources

The following photographs were kindly placed at the disposal of the author, to supplement his own:
Bouvier, Nicolas 44; Bristol, Horace (Sirman) 28, 87, 156; Burri, René 23, 85, 116, 119–121, 123, 125, 128, 134, 143, 153, 154, 186, 190, 202, 204–206, 211, 214–216, 219, 220; Camera Press (Sirman) 45, 138, 165; Eiga, Iwanami (Orion) 5, 9, 13, 24, 31, 35, 57, 66, 111, 113, 114, 117, 172; Hamaya, Hiroshi II, IV, V, 46–48, 147, 173, 175; Japanese Embassy, Berne 61, 192, 195, 200, 209, 212, 222, 228, 229; Japan National Tourist Organization, Tokyo 3, 8, 15, 27, 34, 37, 38, 52, 55, 93, 94, 124, 126, 127, 146, 166, 168, 169, 171, 174, 177–179, 199, 201; Kokusai Bunka Shinkokai, Tokyo 70, 223; Mainichi Shimbun, Tokyo 2, 118; Moritomo, Shinichiro (Orion) 22, 43; Nakada (Sirman) 162; Noguchi, Jun (Orion) 36; Orion Press, Tokyo XI, 21, 39, 40, 148, 167, 217; Orion/Camera Press 11, 12, 203; Ouvehand, Prof. Dr Cornelius 50, 51, 115, 149; Scheidegger, Ernst 16, 18, 20, 130, 132, 133, 136, 137, 189; Service d'Information du Consulat Général du Japon, Geneva 19, 41, 42, 65, 67, 96, 98–100, 102, 131, 164, 176, 181–183, 185, 196–198, 207, 208, 210; Sokagakkai 221; Suzuki, Y. (Sirman) 135; Tajima, Kinnosuke (Orion) 25, 170; Takamasa, Inamura (Sirman) 155; Yamada, Terudo (Orion) 49

The author's grateful thanks are extended not only to all those who have helped him on the photographic side, but also to his friends in Japan, in particular Mrs Momoko Ishi and Mr Tadashi Matsui together with his obliging lady assistants, as well as to Professors Junshiro Wakayama and Cornelius Ouvehand in Zurich, for their encouragement and ready assistance.

Chronological Table

With the traditional roll of emperors (Tenno) and dynastic periods (nengo). The prefix Go signifies the second ruler bearing the name to which it is attached. Of the dates up to about AD 600 only those contained in the Chinese annals have any historical validity. The dates in brackets indicate the life-span, those without brackets the period of rule.

Mythical and Yamato era

Name of the Tenno	Reign	Most important events
1 Jimmu	660–585 BC	
2 Suizei	581–549	
3 Annei	548–511	
4 Itoku	510–477	
5 Kosho	476–393	
6 Koan	392–291	
7 Korei	290–215	
8 Kogen	214–158	
9 Kaika	157–98	
10 Sujin	97–30	First attempts to establish an imperial regime
11 Suinin	29 BC–AD 70	AD 57 First diplomatic mission from daimyo of Nu on Kyushu to China
12 Keiko	71–130	Subjection of the Kumaso on Kyushu and the Ainu in the north
13 Seimu	131–190	
14 Chuai	192–200	
15 Ojin	200–310	200–269 Empress Jingo-Kogo as regent 200 (historically, nearer 363). Invasion of Korea 238 Third diplomatic mission to China 266 Seventh mission to China. Recruitment of Korean and Chinese artisans 284–5 (historically, nearer 404). Introduction of the Chinese script through the Koreans Achiki and Wa-ni
16 Nintoku	313–399	
17 Richu	400–405	
18 Hansho	406–411	
19 Ingyo	412–453	425 The ninth diplomatic mission to China brings the Japanese ruler the title Chiang-chün, Japanese shogun (Great General) from Nanking
20 Anko	454–456	
21 Yuryaku	457–479	478 Seventeenth mission to China. Spread of Chinese culture

22	Seinei		480–484		
23	Kenso		485–487		
24	Ninken		488–498		
25	Buretsu		499–506		
26	Keitai		507–531		
27	Ankan		533–535		
28	Senka		536–539		
29	Kimmei		540–571		552 is recognized as the official date for the introduction of Buddhism
30	Bidatsu		572–585		
31	Yomei		586–587		587 The struggle between the Soga and Monobe clans ends in victory for the pro-Buddhist Soga
32	Sushun		588–592		

From Shotoku Taishi to the Nara Period

33	Suiko, Empress	(554–628)	593–628		Prince Shotoku Taishi (572–621) governs as regent 593–621 600 Twentieth mission to China 607 Twenty-first (first official) mission to China. Far-reaching reforms. Spread of Buddhism. Horiyuji Temple built
34	Jomei	(593–641)	629–641		
35	Kogyoku, Empress	(594–661)	642–645		645 Fall of the Soga

NENGO

36	Kotoku	(596–654)	645–654	Taika 645–650	646 Naka-no-Oe, later Tenno Tenchu, and Nakafomi Kamatari, founder of the Fujiwara dynasty, introduce the Taika reform
37	Saimei, Empress (identical with 35)		655–661	Hakuchi 650–655	655 Dosho imports the Hosso sect from China 670 First referendum
38	Tenchi	(626–671)	662–671		
39	Kobun	(648–672)	672	Sujaku 672	
40	Temmu	(622–686)	673–686	Hakuho 673–686	
41	Jito, Empress	(646–703)	687–696	Shucho 686–701	
42	Mommu	(683–707)	697–707	Taiho; 701–704	701 Law codes: Taiho-Ritsuryo-Ritsu (Penal code) and Ryo (Civil code)
43	Gemmyo, Empress	(662–722)	708–714	Wado 708–715	710 Nara becomes the capital 712 The history book *Kojiki* is completed Poetry anthology *Man-yo-shu*
44	Gensho, Empress regent until 748	(681–748)	715–723	Reiki 715–717 Yoro 717–724	720 The history book *Nihonshoki* is completed
45	Shomu	(699–756)	724–749	Jinki (Shinki) 724–728 Tempyo 729–749 Tempyo-kampo 749	740 Roben founds the Kegon sect 745 The Chinese Ganjin introduces the Ritsu sect

46	Koken, Empress	(718–769)	749–757	Tempyo-shoho	749–757	751 Daibutsu is cast in Nara
47	Junnin	(733–765)	758–764	Tempyo-hoji	757–765	
48	Shotoku, Empress (identical with 46)		765–769	Tempyo-jingo	765–767	
				Jingo-keiun	767–770	769 Fall of the priest-chancellor Dokyo (d. 772) who was given the title of hoo
49	Konin	(719–781)	770–781	Hoki	770–781	
				Ten-o	781–782	

Heian Period 794-1185

50	Kammu	(736–805)	782–805	Enryaku	782–806	794 Heian (Kyoto) becomes capital 805 Dengyo Daishi founds the Tendai sect
51	Heijo	(774–824)	806–809	Daido	806–810	806 On his return from China Kobo Daishi founds the Shingon sect
52	Saga	(785–842)	809–822	Konin	810–824	
53	Junna	(786–840)	823–832	Tencho	824–834	
54	Nimmyo	(810–850)	833–850	Showa (Jowa)	834–848	
				Kasho	848–851	
55	Montoku	(827–858)	851–858	Ninju	851–854	
				Saiko	854–857	
				Ten-an	857–859	858 Fujiwara Yoshifusa (804–872) becomes sessho for his grandson, the Tenno, who is under age
56	Seiwa	(851–881)	859–876	Jogan	859–877	
57	Yozei	(868–949)	877–884	Genkei	877–885	
58	Koko	(830–887)	884–887	Nin-na	885–889	884–891 Motosune Fujiwara (836–891) governs as kampaku. The Fujiwara at the height of their power
59	Uda	(867–931)	888–897	Kampei (Kampyo)	889–898	The poet and statesman Sugawara Michizane (845–903), whom the Tenno Uda had brought in to oppose the Fujiwara, is banished in 898
60	Daigo	(885–930)	898–930	Shotai	898–901	
				Engi	901–923	Age of enlightenment. 918 Fukana Sukohito's work of natural science, *Honzo-Wamyo*, 922 the *Kokin-Wakashu* anthology with songs of the 'Six Genii', appear.
				Encho	923–931	Fujiwara Tadahira (880–949) becomes sessho 941, kampaku 94, dajo-daijin 943
61	Suzaku	(923–952)	931–946	Shohei (Shohyo)	931–938	935 Ki-no-Tsurayuki completes his travel-book *Tosa-nikki* 935 Revolt of the Taira-no-Masakado
				Tenkei (Tengyo)	938–947	
62	Murakami	(926–967)	947–967	Tenryaku	947–957	
				Tentoku	957–961	

				Owa	961–964	
				Koho	964–968	
63	Reizei	(950–1011)	968–969	An-na	968–970	
64	Enyu	(959–991)	969–984	Tenroku	970–973	
				Ten-en	973–976	
				Jogen (Teigen)	976–978	978 Chinese merchants enter into trade relations
				Tengen	978–983	
				Eikan	983–985	
65	Kazan	(968–1008)	984–986	Kan-na	985–987	
66	Ichijo	(980–1011)	986–1011	Eien	987–989	995–1027 Fujiwara Michinaga (966–1027) in power
				Eiso	989–990	
				Shoreki (Shoryaku)	990–995	
				Chotoku	995–999	
				Choho	999–1004	Around 1000 the literary works *Genji-Monogatari* by the lady of the court Murasaki Shikibu and *Makura-no-Soshi* by the lady of the court Sei-Shonagon are produced
				Kanko	1004–1012	
67	Sanjo	(976–1017)	1011–1017	Chowa	1012–1017	
68	Go-Ichijo	(1008–1036)	1017–1036	Kannin	1017–1021	
				Jian (Chian)	1021–1024	
				Manju	1024–1028	1027–1074 Fujiwara Yorimichi (992–1074) governs as kampaku
				Chogen	1023–1037	
69	Go-Suzaku	(1009–1045)	1037–1045	Choreki (Choryaku)	1037–1040	
				Chokyu	1040–1044	
				Kantoku	1044–1046	
70	Go-Reizei	(1025–1068)	1046–1068	Eisho	1046–1053	
				Tenki	1053–1058	
				Kohei	1058–1065	
				Jiryaku (Chiryaku)	1065–1069	
71	Go-Sanjo	(1034–1073)	1069–1072	Enkyu	1069–1074	Following his abdication Go-Sanjo governs on behalf of his son and successor and thereby creates the office of 'in'
72	Shirakawa	(1053–1129)	1073–1086	Shoho (Joho)	1074–1077	
				Shoreki (Joryaku)	1077–1081	
				Eiho	1081–1084	
				Otoku	1084–1087	
73	Horikawa	(1078–1107)	1087–1107	Kanji	1087–1094	
				Kaho	1094–1096	
				Eicho	1096–1097	
				Shotoku	1097–1099	
				Kowa	1099–1104	
				Choji	1104–1106	
				Kasho	1106–1108	
74	Toba	(1103–1156)	1107–1123	Tennin	1108–1110	
				Ten-ei	1110–1113	
				Eikyu	1113–1118	

				Gen-ei	1118–1120	
				Hoan	1120–1124	
75	Sutoku	(1119–1164)	1123–1141	Tenji	1124–1126	
				Daiji (Taiji)	1126–1131	
				Tensho	1131–1132	
				Chosho	1132–1135	
				Hoen	1135–1141	
				Eiji	1141–1142	
76	Konoe	(1139–1155)	1142–1155	Koji	1142–1144	
				Ten-yo	1144–1145	
				Kyuan	1145–1151	
				Nimpei (Nimpyo)	1151–1154	
				Kyuju	1154–1156	
77	Go-Shirakawa	(1127–1192)	1155–1158	Hogen	1156–1159	
78	Nijo	(1143–1165)	1159–1165	Heiji	1159–1160	
				Eiriki (Eiryaku)	1160–1161	
				Oho	1161–1163	
				Chokan	1163–1165	
79	Rokujo	(1164–1176)	1165–1168	Eiman	1165–1166	1167 The Taira under Kiyomori (1118–1181) at the height of their power
				Nin-an	1166–1169	
80	Takakura	(1161–1181)	1168–1180	Kao	1169–1171	
				Shoan (Joan)	1171–1175	
				Angen	1175–1177	1175 Honen Shonin founds the Jodo sect
				Jisho	1177–1181	
81	Antoku	(1178–1185)	1180–1182	Yowa	1181–1182	1180–1185 Gempei war between the Minamoto and the Taira
				Juei	1182–1184	

Kamakura Period 1185–1333

82	Go-Toba	(1179–1239)	1184–1198	Genryaku	1184–1185	1184 Minamoto Yoritomo (1147–1199) introduces military government (bakufu) with headquarters in Kamakura and rules 1192–1199 as shogun
				Bunji	1185–1190	
				Kenkyu	1190–1199	
						1187 Fujiwara-no-Shunzei finishes his poetry anthology *Senzai Waka-shu*
						1191 Eisen returns from China and founds the Rinzai-Zen sect
						Hojo Tokimasa (1138–1215) initiates the power of the Hojo as shiken in 1199
83	Tsuchi-Mikado	(1195–1231)	1198–1210	Shoji	1199–1201	Shogun: Minamoto Yori-ie (1182–1204) 1202–1203
				Kennin	1201–1204	1201–1220 The Imperial Collection of Poetry *Shinkokin Wakashu* produced
				Genkyu	1204–1206	Shogun: Minamoto Sanetomo (1192–1219) 1203–1219
				Ken-ei	1206–1207	

				Shogen (Jogen)	1207–1211	Shiken: Hojo Yoshitoki (1163–1224) 1205–1216 and 1219–1224
84	Juntoku	(1197–1242)	1210–1221	Kenryaku	1211–1213	
				Kempo	1213–1219	Shiken: Hojo Hirotomo 1216–1219
				Shokyu (Jokyu)	1219–1222	
85	Chukyo	(1218–1234)	1221			Shogun: Fujiwara Yoritsume (1244–1256) 1219–1244
86	Go-Horikawa	(1212–1234)	1222–1232	Joo (Tei-o)	1222–1224	
				Gennin	1224–1225	Shiken: Hojo Yasutoki (1183–1242) 1224–1242
				Karoku	1225–1227	1226 Ippen founds the Jishu sect
				Antei	1227–1229	
				Kanki	1229–1232	
87	Shijo	(1231–1242)	1232–1241	Joei (Tei-ei)	1232–1233	
				Tempuku	1233–1234	
				Bunryaku	1234–1235	
				Katei	1235–1238	
				Rekinin (Ryakunin)	1238–1239	
				En-o	1239–1240	
				Ninji	1240–1243	Shiken: Hojo Tsunetoki (1224–1246) 1242–1246
88	Go-Saga	(1220–1272)	1242–1246	Kangen	1243–1247	Shogun: Fujiwara Yoritsuge (1239–1256) 1244–1252
89	Go-Fukakusa	(1243–1304)	1246–1259	Hoji	1247–1249	Shiken: Hojo Tokiyori (1226–1263) 1246–1256
				Kencho	1249–1256	
				Kogen	1256–1257	1252 Daibutsu erected in Kamakura
				Shoka	1257–1259	Shogun: Prince Munetaka (1242–1274) 1252–1266
				Shogen	1259–1260	1253 Nichiren founds the Lotus sect
90	Kameyama	(1259–1305)	1260–1274	Bun-o	1260–1261	
				Kocho	1261–1264	
				Bun-ei	1264–1275	Shogun: Prince Koreyasu (1264–1326) 1266–1289
						Shiken: Hojo Tokimune (1251–1284) 1268–1281
91	Go-Uda	(1267–1324)	1274–1287	Kenji	1275–1278	Mongol invasion of Kyushu repulsed 1274
				Koan	1278–1288	1281 Second Mongol invasion repulsed Shiken: Hojo Sadatoki (1270–1311) 1284–1300
92	Fushimi	(1265–1317)	1288–1298	Sho-o	1288–1293	Shogun: Prince Hisa-akira (1274–1328) 1289–1308
				Einin	1293–1299	
93	Go-Fushimi	(1288–1336)	1298–1301	Shoan	1299–1302	Shiken: Hojo Morotoki 1301–1311
94	Go-Nijo	(1285–1308)	1301–1308	Kengen	1302–1303	
				Kagen	1303–1306	
				Tokuji	1306–1308	
95	Hanazono	(1297–1348)	1308–1318	Enkei	1309–1311	Shogun: Prince Morikuni (1302–1333) 1308–1333
				Ocho	1311–1312	

				Showa	1312–1317	Shiken: Hojo Takatoki (1303–1333)
				Bumpo	1317–1319	1316–1326
96	Go-Daigo	(1287–1338)	1318–1338	Gen-o	1319–1321	
				Genko	1321–1324	
				Shochu	1324–1326	
				Kareki	1326–1329	
				Gantoku	1329–1331	
				Genko	1331–1334	Shogun: Prince Morinaga (1308–1335) 1333–1334

Muromachi Period 1338–1573

Southern Dynasty			*Northern Dynasty*			
96 (Go-Daigo)	Genko	1331–1334	Kogon (1313–1364) 1331–1333	Shokai	1332–1334	Shogun: Price Morinaga (1308–1335) 1333–1334
	Kemmu	1334–1336				Shogun: Prince Nariyoshi (1325–1338) 1334–1336
	Engen	1336–1340	Komyo (1322–1380) 1336–1348	Kemmu Ryaku-o Koei	1336–1338 1338–1342 1342–1345	Ashikaga Takauji (1308–1358) becomes Generalissimo 1335, shogun 1338–1358
97 Go-Murikami (1328–1368) 1339–1368	Kokoku Shohei	1340–1346 1346–1370		Teiwa	1345–1350	
			Suko (1334–1399) 1348–1351	Kan-o	1350–1352	1351 The Imperial Insignia pass to the northern dynasty
			Go-Kogon (1338–1374) 1353–1371	Bunwa	1352–1356	
				Embun	1356–1361	2 Ashikaga-shogun: Yoshiaki (1330–1368)
				Koan	1361–1362	1358–1367
				Teiji (Joji)	1362–1368	3 Ashikaga-shogun: Yoshimitsu (1358–1408) 1368–1394
98 Chokei (?–?) 1368–1372	Kentoku	1370–1372	Go-En-yu (1359–1393) 1372–1382	O-an	1368–1375	
	Bunchu	1372–1375		Eiwa	1375–1379	
99 Go-Kameyama (1347–1424) 1373–1392	Tenju	1375–1381		Koreki (Koryaku)	1379–1381	
	Kowa	1381–1384		Eitoku	1381–1384	
	Genchu	1384–1393	Go-Komatsu (1377–1433) 1383–1412	Shitoku	1384–1387	First flowering of No-drama through Kan-ami (1333–1384) and
				Kakei	1387–1389	
				Ko-o	1389–1390	
				Meitoku	1390–1393	Ze-ami (1363–1444)

1392   *Reunion of northern and southern courts*

100	Go-Komatsu (see Northern Dynasty)		Omei (O-ei)	1394–1428	*4* Ashikaga-shogun: Yoshimochi (1386–1428) 1394–1423
101	Shoko	(1401–1428) 1413–1428			*5* Ashikaga-shogun: Yoshikazu (1407–1425) 1423–1425
102	Go-Hanazono	(1419–1471) 1429–1464	Shocho	1428–1429	
			Eikyo	1429–1441	*6* Ashikaga-shogun: Yoshinori (1394–1441) 1429–1441
			Kakitsu	1441–1444	*7* Ashikaga-shogun: Yoshikatsu (1433–1443) 1442–1443
			Bun-an	1444–1449	
			Hotoku	1449–1452	*8* Ashikaga-shogun: Yoshimasa (1435–1490) 1449–1474
			Kyotoku	1452–1455	
			Kosho	1455–1457	
			Choroku	1457–1460	
			Kansho	1460–1466	
103	Go-Tsuchi-Mikado (1442–1500) 1465–1500		Bunsho	1466–1467	
			Onin	1467–1469	1467 Outbreak of the Onin War between the Hosokawa and the Yamana, which continues into the period of the *sengoku*, i.e. of the Warring Provinces, which lasts until 1568
			Bummei	1469–1487	
			Chokyo	1487–1489	
			Entoku	1489–1492	
			Mei-o	1492–1501	*9* Ashikaga-shogun: Yoshihisa (1465–1489) 1474–1489 *10* Ashikaga-shogun: Yoshitane (1465–1522) 1490–1493 and 1508–1521 Sesshu (1420–1506), outstanding painter in water-colour
104	Go-Kashiwabara (1464–1527) 1501–1526		Bunki	1501–1504	*11* Ashikaga-shogun: Yoshizumi (1478–1511) 1494–1508, for a time together with Yoshitane
			Eisho	1504–1521	
			Tai-ei	1521–1528	
105	Go-Nara	(1497–1557) 1526–1557	Kyoroku	1528–1532	*12* Ashikaga-shogun: Yoshiharu (1501–1550) 1522–1546
			Tembun	1532–1555	1542 Portuguese first introduce fire-arms. Masanobu Kano (1434–1530) and his son Motonobu (1478–1559) found the Kano school of painting which flourishes up to the Edo period
			Koji	1555–1558	*13* Ashikaga-shogun: Yoshiteru (1535–1565) 1546–1565 1549 St Francis Xavier in Kagoshima *14* Ashikaga-shogun: Yoshihide (1564–1568) 1568

Momoyama Period 1568–1600

106	Ogimachi	(1517–1593) 1558–1586	Eiroku	1558–1570	1568 The daimyo Oda Nobunaga (1534–1582) enters Kyoto and sets up a new central military regime
			Genki	1570–1573	
			Tensho	1573–1591	*15* Ashikaga-shogun: Yoshiaki (1537–1597) 1568–1573
107	Go-Yozei	(1571–1617) 1587–1610	Bunroku	1592–1596	1582–1598 Toyotomi Hideyoshi in power. Invasion of Korea
			Keicho	1596–1615	

Tokugawa Ieyasu, sole ruler after Hideyoshi's death, transfers the headquarters of the bakufu to Edo in 1600 and 1603–1605 is the first Tokugawa-shogun, who remains in power until his death in 1616

108	Go-Mizuno-o	(1596–1680)	1611–1629	Genna	1615–1624
				Kwan-ei	1624–1644

2 Tokugawa-shogun: Hidetada (1579–1632) 1605–1623

3 Tokugawa-shogun: Iemitsu (1604–1651) 1623–1651

109	Myosho, Empress	(1623–1696)	1630–1643		

1637–1638 The Shimabara revolt is crushed
1639 Japan officially isolated from the outside world

110	Go-Komyo	(1633–1654)	1643–1654	Shoho	1644–1648
				Keian	1648–1652
				Shoo (Joo)	1652–1655

4 Tokugawa-shogun: Ietsuna (1641–1680) 1651–1680

Haiku poetry brought to perfection by Matsuo Basho (1644–1694). With Moronubu (1618–1694) the 'golden age' of the Japanese woodcut begins.

111	Go-Saiin	(1637–1685)	1655–1662	Meireki	1655–1658
				Manji	1658–1661
				Kambun	1661–1673
112	Reigen	(1654–1732)	1663–1686	Empo	1673–1681
				Tenna	1681–1684

Seki Takakatsu (1642–1708), as Master of the 'wasa', one of the most brilliant mathematicians of the time

5 Tokugawa-shogun: Tsunayoshi (1646–1709) 1680–1709

				Jokyo (Teikyo)	1684–1688
113	Higashiyama	(1675–1709)	1687–1709	Genroku	1688–1704
				Hoei	1704–1711

1709 First comprehensive natural science history, *Yamato-Honzo*, by Kaibara Ekken appears

114	Naka-Mikado	(1702–1737)	1710–1735	Shotoku	1711–1716

6 Tokugawa-shogun: Ienobu (1662–1712) 1709–1712

7 Tokugawa-shogun: Ietsugu (1709–1716) 1713–1716

				Kyoho	1716–1736
115	Sakuramachi	(1720–1750)	1735–1746	Gembun	1736–1741
				Kampo	1741–1744
				Enkyo	1744–1748
116	Momozono	(1741–1762)	1747–1762	Kan-en	1748–1751
				Horeki	1751–1764

8 Tokugawa-shogun: Yoshimune (1684–1751) 1716–1745. Kyoho reform

9 Tokugawa-shogun: Ieshige (1711–1761) 1745–1760

10 Tokugawa-shogun: Ieharu (1737–1786) 1760–1786

117	Go-Sakuramachi, Empress	(1740–1813)	1763–1770	Meiwa	1764–1772
118	Go-Momozono	(1758–1779)	1771–1779	An-ei	1772–1781
119	Kokaku	(1771–1840)	1780–1816	Temmei	1781–1789
				Kansei	1789–1801
				Kyowa	1801–1804
				Bunka	1804–1818

Supremacy of the Grand Chamberlain Tanuma Okisugu 1769–1788

11 Tokugawa-shogun: Ienari (1773–1841) 1786–1837. During his minority until 1793 the regent was Matsudaira Sadanobu
The geographer Ino Tadakata (1745–1818) draws the first scientific map of Japan

120	Ninko	(1800–1846)	1817–1846	Bunsei	1818–1830
				Tempo	1830–1844
				Koka	1844–1848

12 Tokugawa-shogun: Ieyoshi (1793–1853) 1837–1853

121	Komei	(1831–1867) 1847–1867	Kaei	1848–1854	1853 Commodore Perry gives a demonstration of American power
			Ansei	1854–1860	13 Tokugawa-shogun: Iesada (1824–1858) 1853–1858
					1854 Treaties with U.S.A. and Russia
			Man-en	1860–1861	14 Tokugawa-shogun: Iemochi (1846–1866) 1858–1866
			Bunkyu	1861–1864	1860–1861 First Japanese mission to Europe and America
			Genji	1864–1865	1866 Japan admits foreign traders
			Keio	1865–1868	15 Tokugawa-shogun: Yoshinobu (keiki, 1837–1913) 1866–1868

Meiji, Taisho and Showa Period

122	Mutsuhito, posthumous: Meiji (1852–1912) 1868–1912	Meiji	1868–1912	1868 Following the abdication of the shogun, the Tenno takes over power and moves his residence from Kyoto to Tokyo (hitherto Edo). Introduction of the Meiji reforms
				1889 Meiji constitution on Western model
				1894–1895 War with China. Annexation of Formosa
				1902 Treaty of alliance with Great Britain
				1910 Annexation of Korea
123	Yoshihito, posthumous: Taisho (1879–1926)	Taisho	1912–1926	1914 Entry into the First World War
				1915 The 21 Demands to China mark the beginning of the expansionist policy on the mainland
				1923 Tokyo devastated by an earthquake
124	Hirohito (b. 1901), from 1921 regent for his father, since 1926 Tenno	Showa since	1926	1931 Following upon the 'Manchurian Incident' the military take control, and Manchuria, as Manchukuo, becomes a vassal state
				1936 Officers' Revolt
				1937 War declared on China
				7 December 1941 Surprise attack on the U.S. fleet in Pearl Harbor, coupled with campaign of aggrandisement in South East Asia
				June 1942 First reverse in the naval battle off Midway Island
				6 August 1945 Hiroshima is destroyed by an atom bomb
				15 August 1945 Imperial Proclamation about ending the war
				1947 The new Constitution is put into effect
				1951 Peace Treaty of San Francisco, end of U.S. occupation
				1964 Olympiad in Tokyo
				1970 World Exhibition in Osaka

Glossary of Japanese Terms

akindo : merchant class in Tokugawa period

ama = Heaven, Buddhist nun; **amadera** = convents; **Amaterasu** = Heaven-irradiating

amabe : professional group

amado : wooden sliding door, rain-door

bakufu (**baku** = curtain, tent; **fu** = government): Field head-quarters, originally the temporary seat of the commander-in-chief; later used to mean the government of the shogun

bonsai : cultivation of miniature trees

bonseki : landscape of stone and sand on a tray

bugaku : ancient court dance

bugyo : Government Commissioner, title of the Ashikaga shoguns

bujutsu : a samurai style of fencing

buke : knights, warriors, military nobility

bun : understanding, learning

bunjin–ike : a style of flower-arrangement cultivated by the literati in the 18th century

bunraku : a form of puppet-show

bushi = warrior; **bushido** : Way of the knight, code of honour of the samurai

Butsu : Buddha

byobu : folding screen

cha = tea; **chaniwa** : garden connected with a house for the tea-ceremony; **chanoyu** = tea-ceremony; **chashitsu** : room for the tea-ceremony

chigi : crossbeam on the roof-ridge of a Shinto shrine

cho : street

chonin : citizen class in Tokugawa period

chu : centre

chuko : love of children, loyalty to ruler

chummon : inner gate of the temple

chunagon : imperial adviser

dai = great; **Daibutsu** : great Buddha

daimyo : feudal prince of the Tokugawa period

dairi : imperial residence

dajo–daijin : Supreme Government Council

dajo–kan : Imperial Council for Secular Affairs

Do : Way, Teaching (often used as suffix)

emakimono : roll of pictures

engawa : gallery running round exterior of house

eta : lowest class of the population in the Tokugawa period (tanners, executioners)

fu : style

fue : pipe, flute

fusuma : partition, sliding door

futon : blanket, mattress

gaki : unredeemed spirit

gaku : study, teaching

gembuku : 'first donning of adult clothing', coming-of-age celebration

getsu : moon, month

go = a syllable with various meanings. Prefixed to the

name of a ruler it signifies the second in the line. Also the name of a game played with pieces on a board

gojunoto : five-storey pagoda

gongen : Buddhist term for Shinto gods

haiku or **haikai** : poem with 5 + 7 + 5 syllables

hako–niwa : box-garden

han : area of jurisdiction of a daimyo

harakiri : disembowelment, the traditional form of suicide, *see also* seppuku

hatamoto : vassal of the shogun

heimin : citizen class in the Meiji period

hina : doll; **hina matsuri** : Doll Festival (3 March)

hinin = nonentity; beggar in the Tokugawa period

hiragana : later Japanese syllabic script (*c.* AD 900)

hiraniwa : garden in flat landscape

hojo : abbot's quarters in the temple precincts

hoo : King of the Law; title of an abdicated emperor, who has become a monk

hyakusho, abbreviated to **No** : the peasant class in the Tokugawa period

iaijutsu : style of fencing

ie : family

ikebana : art of flower-arrangement

in : Buddhist (subsidiary) temple, often attached as a suffix to the name

Inari : Rice deity, portrayed as a white fox

in–kyo : retirement into private life

in–sei : guardianship or regency of abdicated emperor on behalf of his successor

isshu : kind, type

iwa : rock

ji : temple monastery, as suffix to the name

Jindai : the Age of the Gods

jingikan : Imperial office for Shinto and ancestor worship

jinja : Shinto shrine

jiriki : Buddhist doctrine of self-redemption

joko : father of the emperor, abdicated emperor

jomon (jo = cord, **mon** = pattern) : type of pottery which gave its name to the prehistoric cultural epoch

joruri : ballads set to music, puppet-theatre

judo : popular form of jujitsu

juichii : title of Grand Chamberlain

jujitsu : the art of overcoming an opponent by means of wrestling holds

junrei : pilgrimage

kabuki : stage-play with song and dance

kado : art of flower-arrangement

kagami : mirror

kagura : ancient ritual dance

kai : sea, ocean

kairaishi : puppeteer

kaisando : founder's hall of the temple

kakemono : rolled picture for hanging

kami : deity, spirit

kampaku : regent for the (adult) Tenno

Kan : China

kanji : Chinese script

kannushi : Shinto priest

kanryo : title of the regents of the two government centres in Kyoto and Kamakura in the Muromachi period

kanshitzu : lacquer technique in the Nara period

karamon : Chinese gateway

kara–yo : Tang, or Chinese, style

katakana : the older Japanese syllabic script (Nara period)

katsuogi : crossed round beams in the roof of a Shinto shrine

kawa = river; **Kawa–biraki :** River Festival

kaze : wind

kazoku : the nobility in the Meiji period

ken : province, prefecture

kendo : style of fencing

kenjutsu : samurai style of fencing

kigan : litany

kiko : type of travel account favoured since the *Tosa-nikki* of AD 935

ko signifies, according to the sign used: childlike love, devotion, school. Also abbreviation for **sho–kumin,** artisan class of the Tokugawa period

kodo : prayer-hall of the temple. Also expression for incense-burning

koji : posthumous name

koku : measure for rice (1.8 hectolitres)

kokugaku : Japanese studies

kondo : Golden Hall, main hall of the temple

kongo shinto : combination of Shinto and Buddhism

kori : halo, aureole

Koshi : Confucius

koto : instrument with 13 (originally 6) strings

kuge : Court nobility

kuni : the tribal or village community in ancient Japan

Kwa.. : for words with these initial letters *see* the form **Ka..,** which is more widely used today

kyo : town

kyogen : comic interlude, connected with No.

kyoro : the temple building where the holy scriptures are preserved

kyudo : art of archery

machi : street, city quarter

mageire : style of 'natural' flower-arrangement

makimono : long picture roll with square format

matsu : stone-pine

Meiji : Enlightened Government: nengo and posthumous name of Emperor Mutsuhito

mikado : imperial doorway, the Imperial Court; in Europe the name is popularly applied to the Tenno

miya : Shinto shrine

mizu : water

monogatari : tales

mori : forest

naijin : room in temple containing the idol

namu : glorification (in liturgy)

nan : south

nembutsu : name used in invoking Buddha

nengo : span according to which, since AD 645, historical dates are fixed

nikki : the literary group to which the diaries belong

ninyo : doll

Nippon, originally Nihon: old name for Japan

nushi : master

Obon : Buddhist festival of the dead (July)

ocha : tea

odori : dance

ogoshon : abdicated shogun

O–Haira : Shinto festival of the Great Purification

okomori : religious hermitage

onsen : natural hot springs

raido : ritual hall of the temple complex

rien–jo : letter of divorce dating from the Tokugawa period

rikka : stylized form of flower-arrangement

Risshun : beginning of spring

ritsu : prescription, presentiment

ronin : samurai acknowledging no master

ryo : decree, order, sphere of jurisdiction of a feudal baron

samisen : plucking-instrument with three strings

san : mountain; with a different sign = three

sangi : Imperial State Council

sei : Government

seii daishogun : *see* shogun

seppuku : ritual suicide, more elegant (Chinese) expression for harakiri

sessho : guardian-regent for an emperor not yet of age

setchu–yo : mixed Chinese-indigenous style

Shaka (Sanskrit: Sakyamuri): the historical Buddha

shariden : hall of relics

shi : town (of at least 30,000 inhabitants), history

shibai : theatre, stage

shichi–go–san : seven-five-three: visiting-day at the temple for children of these ages

shiken : regent for a shogun of the Kamakura period

shima or **jima** = island

shin = new; with different signs: vassal, heart, deity

shinden = building of the master (of the house); **shindenzukuri :** architecture of a distinguished dwelling-house

Shinto : Way of the gods

shiro : castle, palace

shishi : resolute men

shizoku, abbrev. **shi :** samurai class

shoden : entry to the Imperial Court

shoen : State properties

shogun, more precisely **seii daishogun :** Supreme Commander for the expulsion of the barbarians (the Ainu and other tribes); since the Kamakura period, the title of the regent

shoin : reception-hall of the temple

shoji : sliding window with paper covering

shokunin, abbrev. **ko :** artisan class in Tokugawa period

shonin, abbrev. **sho :** merchant class in Tokugawa period

Showa = Radiant Peace: nengo of Emperor Hirohito, who has ruled since 1926

shugo : military governor

shuro : bell-tower of the temple precincts

sohei : warrior monks

sono : garden

sonno : worship of the Tenno

soshi : founder's hall in the temple

suibokuga : black-and-white ink drawing

sukiya : tea-house for the tea-ceremony

sumo : Japanese wrestling

tahoto : round temple-tower with square base

taika : title of abdicated kampaku

tairo : most senior Minister in Tokugawa period

takusen : oracle

tana : wall-ledge for books, etc.

Tanabata : Festival of the Stars (July)

Tango–no–Sekku : Boys' Festival, today a general children's festival (5 May)

tariki : redemption through Amida

tatami : straw mats for letting into the floor (*c.* 70 × 35 in.)

tategu : sliding door or window

Tempyo = Heavenly Peace, name of a nengo

ten–chi–jin = heaven-earth-man: style of flower arrangement

Tenno, also **Tenshi, Tenson :** Emperor's title

tenryo : the shogun's estates

tenshu : main tower of the castle

tera : Buddhist temple

to : pagoda

toko = niche; **tokonoma :** picture-niche in a room

torii : arched gateway of a Shinto shrine

tsuitate : mounted umbrella

tsukimi : contemplating the moon

tsukiyama : garden in hilly landscape

tsuzumi : hand-drum

ubuya : maternity hut (from antiquity)

uji = clan in old Japan; **ujigami :** ancestor and tutelary god of the clan

uta or **yokyoku :** text of the No play

Wa : Chinese name for Japan

wa–yo : indigenous (as opposed to the Chinese) style

yabusame : archery from a galloping horse

yama : mountain

yamatoe : Japanese painting

yashiki : elegant house

yashiro : Shinto shrine

yumedono : dream-hall of the temple complex

yurei : spirit

za : seat, chair, role, theatre

zaibutsu : term designating the leading family-owned industrial concerns up to 1945

zengakuren : modern movement of radical students of the Left

The spelling of Japanese names used throughout this book conforms with current usage, simplified by the omission of stress-marks above vowels, a method adopted in the most recent edition of the New York Official Guide issued by the Japan National Tourist Organization.

INDEX

Numerals in bold type refer to the black-and-white plates